Look Mom! I Built My Own Web Site

Read the Reviews! (First edition)

★★★★★ Excellent!

Detra Fitch TOP 500 REVIEWER

"This is an EXCELLENT guide for beginners!"

★★★★★ Websites made simple...

Kurt Messick TOP 50 REVIEWER

"Another great advantage of the book is that it is practical - it doesn't spend a lot of time on theory, but rather gives short, easy to understand instructions for how to do basic things."

★★★★☆ Nice starting point of learning...

Manuel J Hernandez TOP 100 REVIEWER

"If you take away the "Look what I did, Mom!" factor, it may also work as a very basic reference for HTML newbies in general (young and old)."

★★★★★ Friendly And Useful

John G. Hilliard, Amazon TOP 100 REVIEWER

"It gives the reader a nice step by step process that is not intimidating."

★★★★☆ Colorful, accessible, fun

David Karlins, Web design author and consultant

"Explanations are clear, complete (in the context of a book for young children), and accurate."

★★★★★ Instruction manual for creating a website

Midwest Book Review

"This book is highly recommended for anyone at any age who wants to have a website of their own for any purpose!"

★★★★★ Youngsters Can Create Their Own Web Sites

William E. Dillane "Bill Dillane"

"This is an excellent book for youngsters and even adults."

★★★★★ A valuable tool for kids...and adults alike
Chris Salzer

"Highly recommended for all beginners looking to get the ball rolling on your very own website!"

★★★★☆ actually bang out HTML
W Boudville

"Amihud gives a young reader a lively and encouraging push into making your own presence on the Web."

★★★★★ Prefect gift that special young web designer
Thomas M. Archer, C# best-selling author

"This book covers everything the young Web designer needs to create their first site and does it with clear, yet non-patronizing, language."

"This book provides an excellent foundation in the fundamentals of web page design written especially for children."
John Gilson, www.htmltutorials.ca

"This is an excellent, easy-to-follow book with great examples and ample illustrations."
Susan Johnson, MyShelf.com

"Look Mom! I Built My Own Web Site is primarily designed for young teenagers (ages 11 to 17), but anyone wanting to build a personal Web site can definitely benefit."
Cheryl McCann, www.review-books.com

"Takes you straight to the core fundamentals of site creation..."
Phillip Kerman, Flash author, teacher www.phillipkerman.com

"A valuable addition to any library of books on building web sites."
Jesse Liberty, www.libertyassociates.com

"The information is applicable to anyone who wants to build a personal site."
Kathleen A. Nester, School Library Journal

Look Mom!
I built my own Web site

Second Edition

Zohar Amihud

If you built your own Web site with the help of this book and offer it on the Internet, please let us know. Send an e-mail to **info@bookchamp.net**, with your name, the state and city where you live, your age and the link to your Web site.

We will review your site and may decide to put a link to it from the book's Web site, if it fulfills all the requirements.

Good luck!

BookChamp

Fords, NJ

Look Mom! I built my own Web site, Second Edition

ISBN-10: 0-9760111-1-5
ISBN-13: 978-0-9760111-1-8

LCC – Library of Congress Catalog Card Number: 2005909206

Printed in Israel
First Printing: September 2006

Trademarks

All terms, products and company names in this book that are known to be trademarks or service marks have been appropriately capitalized. BookChamp cannot attest to the accuracy of this information. Use of a term in this book should not be regarded as affecting the validity of any service or any trademark.

Warning and Disclaimer

The author and publisher have made every effort in the preparation of this book to ensure the accuracy of the information. However, the information contained in this book and/or in the companion Web site is presented without warranty, either express or implied. Neither the author, BookChamp, nor its dealers or distributers will be held liable for any damages caused or alleged to be caused either directly or indirectly by the use of the information and/or code contained in this book or in the companion Web site.

Managing Editor: Sara Amihud

Cover Design: Sharon Raz

Published by: BookChamp
605 King Georges Post Rd.
Fords, NJ 08863
www.bookchamp.net

Distributed by: IPG – Independent Publishers Group
814 North Franklin St.
Chicago, IL 60610
www.ipgbook.com

Contents

Contents

If you're not on the Net, you don't exist! This goes for surfing, for e-mail as well as for building your own Web site.

If you feel you have something to say, a topic to discuss, or you just want to share your creativity and/or make some kind of contribution to the community, all you need to do is build and publish a Web site. Through your site you can reach more people than would be possible through any other publicity medium you can think of – and all for FREE! In almost no time you can be out there, with your own site on the World Wide Web – and yes, folks, it is absolutely **FREE OF CHARGE!**

This book explains how to build a Web site directly and clearly, in plain English, and it makes it easy for anyone to read, follow and understand. Practical examples provide a useful tool to help understand new ideas.

Is this book for you?

◎ If you like to surf, send and receive e-mail, but do not have your very own Web site yet, this is the perfect book to get you started!

◎ If you really want to build your own Web site, but all those heavyweight, serious books scare you off, this is the right book for you!

◎ If you have already built your Web site and so far it is only on your home PC or your school computer, but you really want to put it out there on the Net – this book will show you how! Right now, only a small number of people can access your site – not because it is classified or blocked in any way, but because it exists only on a stand-alone computer or an internal school network. This book will give you the information you need to find the right hosting server to store your special Web site. And all of this comes to you FREE (well, at least most of it!).

◎ If you have built your Web site and already stored it with a free server, but you would really like to know more about how and where to store your site on the Internet – you'll find everything you need right here in this book. You will discover lots of new and interesting information.

This book instructs non-professional computer users on how to build a personal Web site and how to put it on the Net.

What this book covers

This book instructs teenagers and non-professional computer users on how to build a personal Web site for FREE, combining step-by-step simple instructions with practical and entertaining examples. It first shows how to build a demo site of a virtual person using material from a companion Web site. Then it explains how to customize the Web site, how to make it personal, and finally how to place your site on the Net.

Let's suppose that you are planning to build a Web site that will include: a forum, a chat, a survey, a database, an electronics and video store, flash presentations, Java programs – in short, a site that will do everything except make ice cream! But… when you build anything, anything at all, you have to start from the **foundations**, not the 3rd floor, right? The same goes for a Web site. You will begin with the **basics** that provide you with a strong, broad base on which you will be able to build whatever services you choose and expand them at any time in the future.

The book's Web site

You can find the source code for all the examples presented here on a special site designed only for use with this book:

www.bookchamp.net/lookMom.html

About the author

Zohar Amihud has written a number of books and contributed to other books covering HTML, JavaScript, ASP, ASP.NET, Visual Basic, C# and Microsoft Office. Zohar holds an MCP (Microsoft Certified Professional) certification and has a Master degree in Business Administration in Marketing & Information Technology. When he's not writing, Zohar is probably in the fitness club doing spinning, weight training or running a treadmill.

Acknowledgment

Thanks to Amit Amihud, my older son (12), for spending hours reading this material, pointing out things he did not understand in the text and points I needed to clarify and simplify.

Thanks to the children:
Shahaf Meir (10), Keshet Meir (10), Shon Shchory (12),
Dor Harris (12½), Hadar Shpivak (13), Rina Reim (13½)
I have learned a lot from you.

Thanks to Steve Sander, Gideon Fischler, Tamir Berger, Karen Saltiel , John Gilson, Elisabeth Grace Roberts and Dani Herzbrun for helping me make this book a better one.

Need help?

We ask you to please consider the following points before requesting help:

◎ Please research your question thoroughly. Many of your questions (and answers, too) can probably be found somewhere in the book.

◎ Please check the syntax of the HTML tags. An awful lot of requests for help are about this issue.

◎ Please make your questions as precise as possible. Note the page number you are referring to in the book.

◎ If you have written code that is causing you an error, please include the code (HTML file(s) and image file(s)).

e-mail: support@bookchamp.net

Show us your Web site

If you built your own Web site with the help of this book and offer it on the Internet, please let us know.

Send an e-mail to **info@bookchamp.net**, with your name, the state and city where you live, your age and the link to your Web site.

We will review your site and may decide to put a link to it from the book's Web site, if it fulfills all requirements or if we find it fit.

Tell us what you think

We value your opinion and want to know what we are doing right and what we could do better.

When you write, please be sure to include the following information: the title of the book, page number, line number, what is written and what should be written.

We will carefully review your comments and try to incorporate your suggestions into future books and into the next revision of this same volume.

e-mail: support@bookchamp.net

Mail: BookChamp
605 King Georges Post Rd.
Fords, NJ 08863

Part I
Building a Web site

How to Begin Building a Personal Web Site

In this book, I will provide you with a complete example of how to build a Web site, step by step. It is very important that you follow the instructions closely and precisely. I'm sure you will come up with some creative ideas of your own as you work, and you will probably want to deviate from the instructions in the book. Stop! Don't! You will have a chance to put your own ideas into practice, but not just yet. The first thing is to build a Web site according to the instructions provided in the book. Once you have done that – then the sky is the limit!

Why a personal Web site?

In order to build a Web site you must first choose a subject. Your Web site can be about Britney Spears, Christina Aguilera or Karl Malone. Maybe a Web site about dogs, cats or monkeys. Or your favorite TV soap or sitcom (Friends, Will & Grace, Fear Factor…). Even subjects such as gardening, vegetarian food, the Grand Canyon, the Los Angeles Lakers, horse riding, judo, wine, Mexican food, Pokemons are interesting – the possibilities are endless. The trouble is that if the sample Web site is about dogs, for instance, there will always be someone who will wonder: "Why you did not build a Web site about cats?" And if the sample Web site is about the Cincinnati Reds, someone else will want to know: "Why not about the New York Knicks?" And so on and so forth.

That is the reason we are going to create your sample Web site your own personal Web site, all about **you,** your life, your environment, your hobbies and more.

The demo Web site provided applies to Web sites of all topics.

Remember! **You need to follow the step-by-step procedure provided to build your Web site**.

Mom and Dad

Building a personal Web site is a great opportunity for your parents to be really involved with you and your ideas and to be your partners in the actual process of making the Web site (if you want them to, naturally). They will probably have some suggestions of their own and it might be worth listening to them.

Materials

All the materials you need to build a personal Web site (text and images) can be downloaded from the book's Web site at:

www.bookchamp.net/lookMom.html

Note

Images include: pictures, icons, cliparts, graphics, etc...

The text portions and images you need for building your personal Web site can be found on this book's Web site under the chapter headings.

You are probably wondering how could the text and images of my personal Web site find their way onto the Internet, without anyone asking my permission or taking my picture?

Well, I'll tell you the truth – the personal Web site you are going to build is about a "virtual" boy.

It is not really a personal Web site in the sense that it's a Web site about you. You can change the text portions and the images as you like during the building process, but before you change, add or take away anything, please follow the instructions **exactly** as they are laid out.

The texts and the images that you will download are for practice purposes only.

Before you begin

What you will need:

◎ Personal computer (PC)

◎ Windows 9x/ME/2000/XP operating system

◎ Internet browser:

> Microsoft Internet Explorer 🅔 browser
>
> or Mozilla Firefox 🌐 browser

◎ Microsoft Windows Explorer 📁

◎ Microsoft Notepad text editor 📝

Where can I find these programs?

Text Editor 📝

A **Text Editor** like **Notepad**, that can be found on any Windows operating system, can be used. For:

Windows 9x/ME: Click the **Start** button, choose **Programs**, select **Accessories**, and then select **Notepad**

Windows 2000/XP: Click the **Start** button, choose **All Programs**, select **Accessories**, and then select **Notepad**

Note
*If you did not find Notepad, do not worry. Notepad is a part of Windows, so it is installed in your computer. Try this: Click the **Start** button, choose **Run**, type **notepad** in the window, and then select **OK**.*

Internet browser

1. Start your internet browser: **Internet Explorer** or **Firefox** 🌐

2. From the menu bar, choose **Help**, select **About....**

   Next to the word **Version**, you will see the number of your version.

3. Write down the version number: _____

4. Close the window.

I recommend that you have the latest version. For more information please go to http://www.microsoft.com/ie or http://www.mozilla.org.

Note

*From now on we will shorten the name Internet Explorer to **IE** and Firefox to **FF**.*

Note

Firefox is not a built-in part of Windows. So, if you did not install it, do not warry - use Internet Explorer.

Windows Explorer

Windows 9x/ME: Click the **Start** button, choose **Programs** and then select **Windows Explorer**.

Windows 2000/XP: Click the **Start** button, choose **All Programs** and then select **Windows Explorer**.

Or

press the 🪟 + **E** keys together. First press the 🪟 key (located between Alt and Ctrl) and hold it down, then lightly press the **E** key (located directly beneath the number keys 3 and 4 at the top of the keyboard). Only then release the 🪟 key.

File extensions

To create Web pages easily, you must be sure that you can see the File extensions when you are working in Windows Explorer. Follow the instructions you see according to your operating system.

Identifying your operating system

1. Click the **Start** button.

   The name of your operating system is written vertically next to the menu.

2. Write the name of your operating system here:
   Windows_____

And if you didn't find it, please try this:

1. Double click the **My Computer** icon on your desktop.

2. From the My Computer menu bar, choose **Help**, **About Windows**.

3. Write the name of your operating system here:
   Windows_____

4. Click **OK** to close the window.

And if you still didn't find it, you may try this:

1. Right-click with the mouse (using your right mouse button to click instead of the more commonly used left mouse button) on the **Start** button and choose **Explore**.

2. From the menu bar, choose **Help**, **About Windows**.

3. Write the name of your operating system here:
   Windows_____

4. Click **OK** to close the window.

Please follow the next procedure according to your operating system.

Windows 95

1. Open **Windows Explorer** 📁.
2. From the **View** menu, select **Options**.
3. In the **Options** window, click the **View** tab.
4. Make sure that the **Hide MS-DOS file extensions** check box is not highlighted.
5. Click **OK**.
6. Close **Windows Explorer**.

Windows 98

1. Open **Windows Explorer** 📁.
2. From the **View** menu, select **Folder Options**.
3. In the **Folder Options** window, click the **View** tab.
4. In the **Files and Folders** group, make sure that the **Hide file extensions** check box is not highlighted.
5. Click **OK**.
6. Close **Windows Explorer**.

Windows ME

1. Open **Windows Explorer** 📁.
2. From the **Tools** menu, select **Folder Options**.
3. In the **Folder Options** window, click the **View** tab.
4. In the **Files and Folders** group, make sure that the **Hide file extensions** check box is not highlighted.
5. Click **OK**.
6. Close **Windows Explorer**.

Windows 2000

1. Open **Windows Explorer** .

2. From the **Tools** menu, select **Folder Options**.

3. In the **Folder Options** window, click the **View** tab.

4. In the **Files and Folders** group, make sure that the **Hide file extensions** check box is not highlighted.

5. Click **OK**.

6. Close **Windows Explorer**.

Windows XP

1. Open **Windows Explorer** .

2. From the **Tools** menu, select **Folder Options**.

3. In the **Folder Options** window, click the **View** tab.

4. In the **Files and Folders** group, make sure that the **Hide file extensions** check box is not highlighted.

5. Click **OK**.

6. Close **Windows Explorer**.

CHAPTER 2

Writing Your First Web Page

In the previous chapter you have located the programs you needed to build your own Web site, fixed the file extensions and now you are ready to start.

In this chapter you will build your first Web page.

At the end of this chapter your Web page will look as follows:

As you see, it is still empty (without any content) but it is YOURS!!!

Creating a new folder

1. Open **Windows Explorer**.

   Windows 9x/ME: Click the **Start** button, choose **Programs**, **Windows Explorer**

   Windows 2000/XP: Click the **Start** button, choose **All Programs**, **Windows Explorer**

   Or

   Press the ⊞ + **E** keys together. First press the ⊞ key (located between Alt and Ctrl) and hold it down, then lightly press the **E** key (located directly beneath the number keys 3 and 4 at the top of the keyboard). Only then release the ⊞ key.

2. From the menu bar, choose **View**, **Details**.

3. In the left pane of the window (the left side of the window) click once on the **C:** drive.

4. In the right pane of the window (the right side of the window), right-click with the mouse (using your right mouse button to click instead of the more commonly used left mouse button), and from the pop-up menu (shortcut menu), choose **New**, **Folder** (see figure 2.1).

5. In the right pane of the window, if the **New Folder** is selected (highlighted), type **justin** and then press **Enter**.

   If the **New Folder** is not selected (highlighted), highlight it, right-click with the mouse. From the pop-up menu (shortcut menu) choose **Rename**, type **justin** and then press **Enter**.

6. Open the folder **justin** by double-clicking on the name **justin**.

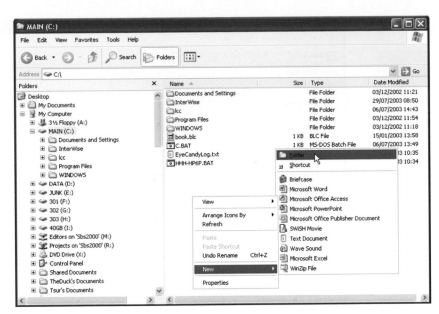

Figure 2.1: *Creating a new folder*

Creating a new Web page

1. In the right pane of the window (which at this stage is now empty), right-click with the mouse. From the pop-up menu, select **New**, **Text Document** (see figure 2.2).

2. Make sure that the new document, which is currently called **New Text Document**.txt, is selected (highlighted). Type **about**.html and then press **Enter**.

   If the **New Text Document.txt** is not selected (highlighted), highlight it, right-click with the mouse. From the pop-up menu choose **Rename**, type **about.html** and then press **Enter**.

3. Note the change in the name of the file extension from **.txt** to **.html**. A message will appear asking if you wish to change the file name extension. Click **Yes**.

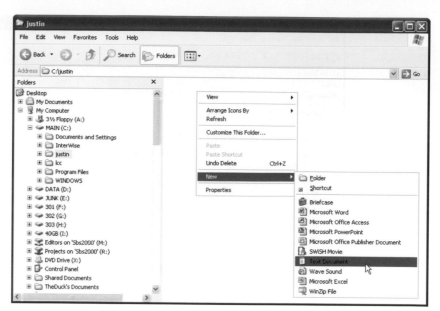

Figure 2.2: Creating a new Text Document.

Note
*The extensions **.html** and **.htm** are the same. In this book I decided to use **.html** as the extension name for a Web page.*

Opening your Web page in the browser

Open **about.html** by double-clicking on it (double or single clicking depending on the Windows definition you have). The Internet browser will open and so will the file (**about.html**) within it. You will see nothing in it at this stage because the file **about.html** is empty.

Viewing the source code of the HTML page

Return to Windows Explorer, highlight the file **about.html,** right-click with the mouse and choose **Open With**, and then choose **Notepad**. **Notepad** will open, but you will see nothing in it because the file **about.html** is still empty.

Note
If you do not see Notepad on the Open With list, select Choose Program..., roll down until you see Notepad, highlight it and click OK.

Writing a basic Web page

1. Type this:

```
<html>
  <head>
    <title>About</title>
    <meta http-equiv="content-type"
      content="text/html;charset=iso-8859-1" />
  </head>
<body>


</body>
</html>
```

2. From the **Notepad** menu bar, select **File** and then select **Save** to save your work.

This is the basic structure of all Web pages that you will create from now on.

Tags are used to tell the browser how to display the Web page content. They are the most basic commands on which the writing of Web pages is based.

<html> tag

The first tag in an HTML file is <html> and the end tag </html> is the final one. All the other tags are written between these two tags.

<head> tag

The opening <head> tag and the closing </head> tag define the title of the Web page. Text within this definition contains information that is not displayed on the browser content pane.

`<title> .... </title>`	Web page title
`<meta />`	Contains more information about the Web page

`<title>` tag

The Web page name will appear in between the `<title>` and the `</title>` tags. It is a good idea to give each Web page a name that describes it as well and as clearly as possible.

Tip
The name of each Web page is also the title that will appear at the top of the browser window. It is important to give a lot of thought to the name of the Web page. Remember that when the user adds your Web page to his favorite list, it will be added by the text between `<title>` and `</title>`.

`<meta />` tag

This tag tells the browser some information about the document you created, including the language it is written in.

```
<meta http-equiv="Content-Type"
  content="text/html;charset=iso-8859-1" />
```

Note
There is a space between the quotation mark (") and the slash symbol (/)

Why iso-8859-1?

In order to display a Web page, the browser has to identify the language it was written in: Turkish, Japanese, Korean, Greek, Hebrew or English. If you do not write the `<meta />` tag (as shown above), the browser may make a mistake in identification, and display the Web page in a different language, one you did not intend, such as Chinese. To force Internet Explorer to display the Web page in **English**, you must write **iso-8859-1**.

Note

The order of the `<title>` *and* `<meta />` *tags does not matter, as long as they come between the* `<head>` *and* `</head>` *tags. In other words, the following is OK:*

```
<head>
  <title>The Title of Your Page</title>
  <meta http-equiv="Content-Type"
  content="text/html;charset=iso-8859-1" />
</head>
```

And so is the following:

```
<head>
  <meta http-equiv="Content-Type"
  content="text/html;charset=iso-8859-1" />
  </title>The Title of Your Page</title>
</head>
```

Every HTML tag must have an opening tag and a closing tag. For instance, the tag `<body>` has the closing tag `</body>`. Some tags have no closing tags, such as `<meta>`. In that case the content of the tag ends with space / and >.

Important Tips:

◎ After an opening tag appears, an appropriate closing tag should also appear. The closing tag is identical to the opening one, except for the addition of the **(/)** symbol. For instance, the title of the Web page is between the opening tag `<title>` and the closing tag `</title>`.

◎ Tags that have no closing tag (like the `meta` tag) should end with a space / followed by >

◎ There is no need to leave spaces between tags, or when pressing the **Enter** key (the browser ignores line breaks that you made in Notepad by pressing **Enter**). Wherever there are several spaces in sequence, the browser treats them as a single space. At this stage you do not yet know how to control spaces, so you should just let the browser do the work for you.

Viewing a Web page in the browser

1. Use the **Taskbar** to bring the browser window to the front. The Taskbar is at the bottom of the display (screen) and includes buttons – one button for each application that is currently open. At this stage the following applications/programs are open: Windows Explorer, Notepad, and Internet browser.

2. From the browser standard buttons toolbar, click the **Refresh\ Reload** button to view the changes you made in **about.html**.

On the browser window heading, you will see the word **About**, which you wrote as part of the `<title>` tag (figure 2.3).

The content pane will remain empty (white).

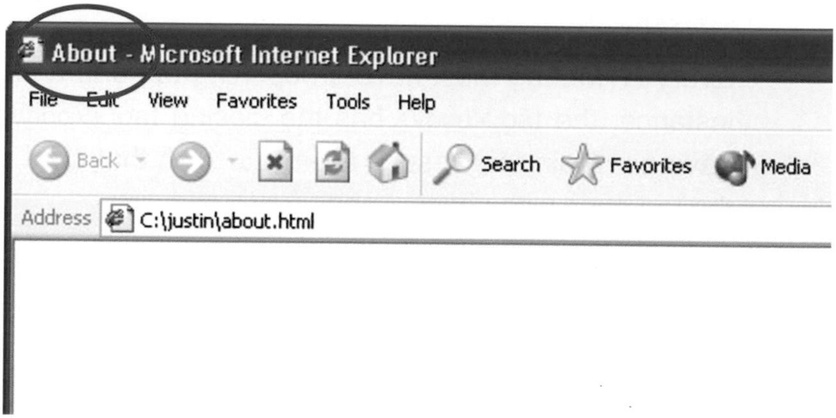

*Figure 2.3: This is how the browser displays the **about.html** file.*

3. Close the browser window where the **about.html** file is displayed.

4. Close the Notepad window where the **about.html** file is displayed.

Playing with Text

In the previous chapter you created the infrastructure for the first HTML page of Justin's web site. This was the **about.html** page.

In this chapter you will:

◎ Add some content and format it into the Web page you have already created (about.html).

◎ Build a new Web page with content (homePage.html).

At the end of this chapter your Web pages will look as follows:

Formatting headings and paragraphs

Viewing an HTML file in the browser

1. Open **Windows Explorer**.

   Windows 9x/ME: Click the **Start** button, choose **Programs**, **Windows Explorer**

   Windows 2000/XP: Click the **Start** button, choose **All Programs**, **Windows Explorer**

   Or

   Press the + **E** keys together. First press the ⊞ key (located between Alt and Ctrl) and hold it down, then lightly press the **E** key (located directly beneath the number keys 3 and 4 at the top of the keyboard). Only then release the ⊞ key.

2. Go to the **justin** folder on drive **C**, where the HTML page named **about.html** is located.

3. Double click on the file **about.html** to view it in the browser.

Note

Internet browser *is abbreviated to* **browser**.

Viewing the source code of the HTML page

Return to Windows Explorer, highlight the file **about.html,** right-click with the mouse and choose **Open With**, and then choose **Notepad**. **Notepad** will open.

Note

If you do not see Notepad on the Open With list, select Choose Program..., roll down until you see Notepad, highlight it and click OK.

By keeping the HTML file open in both the Notepad (text editor) and the browser, you can easily create and view the changes.

Typing the content

1. In Notepad, position the cursor on the empty line following the `<body>` tag. Everything you type between the `<body>` tag and the `</body>` tag will appear in the browser window in the content pane (see figure 3.1).

2. Now continue proceed to type the text. You can either type the following text (press the **Enter** key only where told to do so) or download it from the book's Web site at **www.bookchamp.net/lookMom.html**. Click **Chapter 3** on the left menu. Instructions for using the text are available on the Web site under **Help**.

About `Enter`

My name is Justin and I have a really cool baseball card collection. I'm a fifth-grade student at the George Washington Elementary School in New York. `Enter`

I built a personal web site where you can find information about me, my hobbies, my family and my friends. `Enter`

I was helped by the book Look Mom! I built my own Web site. `Enter`

```
about.html - Notepad
File  Edit  Format  View  Help
<html>
  <head>
    <title>About</title>
    <meta http-equiv="content-type"
      content="text/html;charset=iso-8859-1" />
  </head>
<body>
About
My name is Justin and I have a really cool baseball card collection. I'm
a fifth-grade student at the George Washington Elementary School in
New York.
I built a personal Web site where you can find information about me,
my hobbies, my family and my friends.
I was helped by the book Look Mom! I built my own Web site.
</body>
</html>
```

Figure 3.1: This is how the text you typed in Notepad looks (about.html file).

You will find a lot of examples in this book. You can copy the source code of all the examples from the book's Web site:

www.bookchamp.net/lookMom.html

The examples for each chapter are found in the book's Web site on a page bearing the number of that chapter.

Note:

◎ The <u>full</u> source code of all the examples in the book can be downloaded from the book's Web site.

◎ Sometimes only part of the source code appears in the book, therefore you will need to check the full source code that you downloaded from the book's Web site.

◎ All the examples were checked and run with:
Microsoft Internet Explorer browsers: versions 5.x and 6.x .
Firefox browser: version 1.0.6 .

3. Save the changes you made in the **about.html** file.

Viewing an HTML file in the browser

4. Use the Taskbar to open the browser window.

5. Click the **Refresh\Reload** button to view the changes you made in the **about.html** page, as follows:

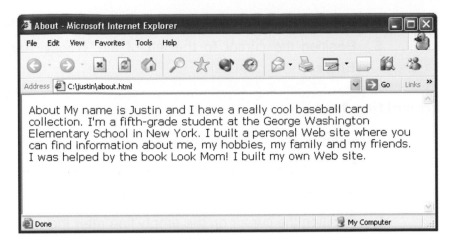

Figure 3.2: This is how the browser displays the about.html file.

Note

If you see letters in a different style, this is because of the browser definitions on your computer.

Does the text look the way you intended it to look? (please circle your answer) Yes / No

The page does not look good in the browser, because the line breaks in the text editor are meaningless in HTML.

6. Go to the **Notepad** window where the **about.html** file is displayed.

Preparing empty lines for writing tags

1. Position the cursor ⌐ to the left (before) of the **About** text and press **Enter.** A new empty line will open.

2. Position the cursor to the left of the **My name** text and press **Enter**.

3. Position the cursor to the left of the **I Built** text and press **Enter**.

4. Position the cursor to the left of the **I was** text and press **Enter**.

5. Position the cursor to the left of the `</body>` tag and press **Enter**.

Formatting text

Formatting the word "About" as a heading – Level 1

1. Position the cursor on the empty line before the word **About,** and type `<h1>`

2. Position the cursor on the empty line after the word **About,** and type `</h1>`

3. Press **Enter**.

Formatting the first paragraph

1. Position the cursor on the empty line before the first paragraph that begins with the text **My Name**, and type `<p>`

2. Position the cursor on the empty line between the first and second paragraphs, and type `</p>`

3. Press **Enter**.

Formatting the second paragraph

1. Type `<p>`

2. Position the cursor on the empty line between the second and third paragraphs, and type `</p>`

3. Press **Enter**.

Formatting the third paragraph

1. Type `<p>`

2. Position the cursor on the empty line after the third paragraph, and type `</p>`

3. Press **Enter**.

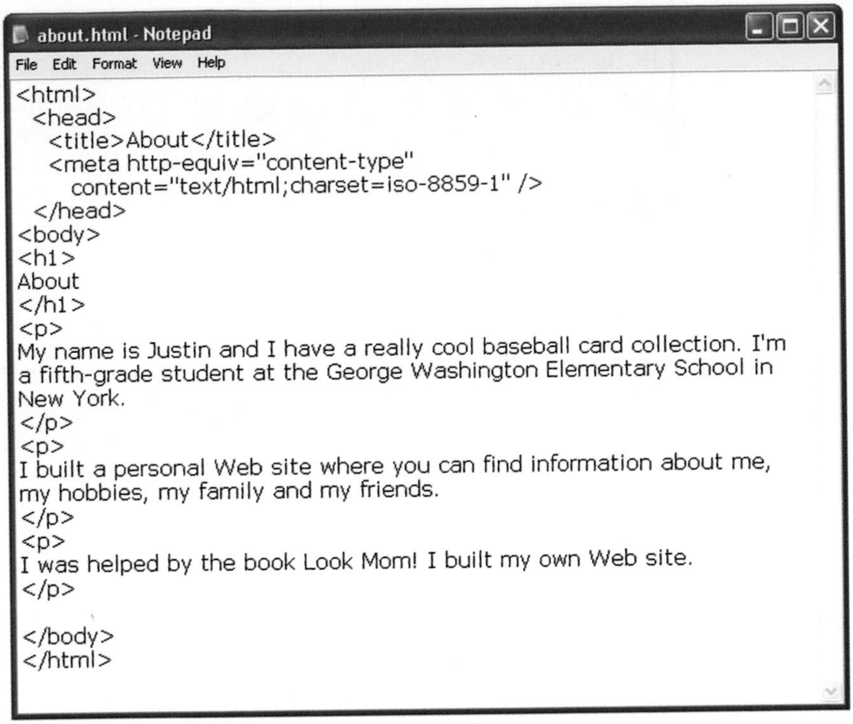

```
about.html - Notepad

File  Edit  Format  View  Help

<html>
  <head>
    <title>About</title>
    <meta http-equiv="content-type"
      content="text/html;charset=iso-8859-1" />
  </head>
<body>
<h1>
About
</h1>
<p>
My name is Justin and I have a really cool baseball card collection. I'm
a fifth-grade student at the George Washington Elementary School in
New York.
</p>
<p>
I built a personal Web site where you can find information about me,
my hobbies, my family and my friends.
</p>
<p>
I was helped by the book Look Mom! I built my own Web site.
</p>

</body>
</html>
```

*Figure 3.3: This is how the **about.html** file in Notepad will appear after the paragraph tags have been inserted.*

Saving and viewing the changes

1. From **Notepad** menu bar, select **File** and then select **Save** to save your work.

2. Use the **Taskbar** to bring the browser window to the front. The Taskbar is at the bottom of the display (screen) and includes buttons – one button for every application that is currently open.

3. From the browser standard buttons toolbar, click the **Refresh\ Reload** button to reload the page and to view the changes you made in **about.html** (as shown in figure 3.4).

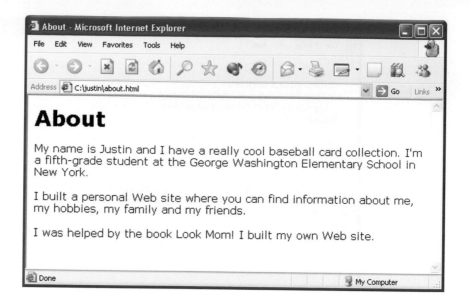

Figure 3.4: The **about.html** file formatted into paragraphs.

There are six levels of headings: h1, h2, h3, h4, h5 and h6. Each heading level is displayed by the browser in a different font size, so that the size of the h4 heading is different from the h1 heading.

Note

The header information of the Web page is in the <header> tag. The tags: <h1>, <h2> . . . are used to format text. Do not be confuse between these two "headers"

The <p> . . . . </p> tags mark the boundaries of a section of text and define it as a paragraph, making it both convenient to handle and more attractive to look at.

Bold format

Bold text

1. Go to the **Notepad** window where the content of the **about.html** file is displayed.

2. Place the cursor to the left of (i.e. before) the **Justin** text.

3. Type <b>

4. Place the cursor the right of (i.e. after) the **Justin** text.

5. Type </b>

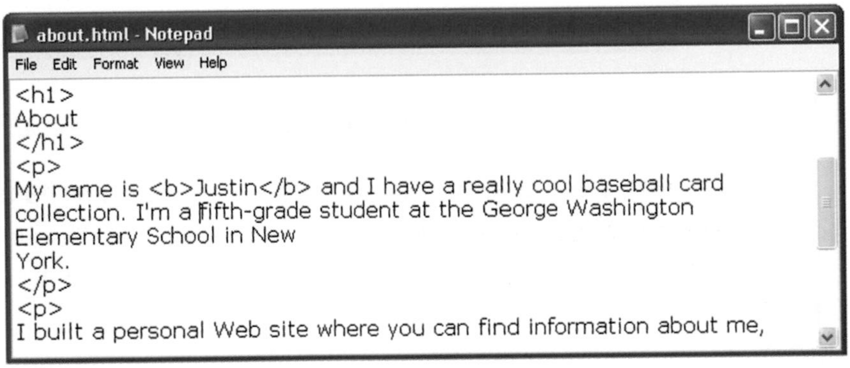

```
about.html - Notepad

File  Edit  Format  View  Help

<h1>
About
</h1>
<p>
My name is <b>Justin</b> and I have a really cool baseball card
collection. I'm a fifth-grade student at the George Washington
Elementary School in New
York.
</p>
<p>
I built a personal Web site where you can find information about me,
```

Figure 3.5: The text Justin is "surrounded" by the <b> and </b> tags.

You have just completed formatting the **Justin** text.

6. Save the changes that you made in the **about.html** file.

7. Go to the browser window and click the **Refresh\Reload** button to view the changes that you made in the **about.html** file (as shown in figure 3.6).

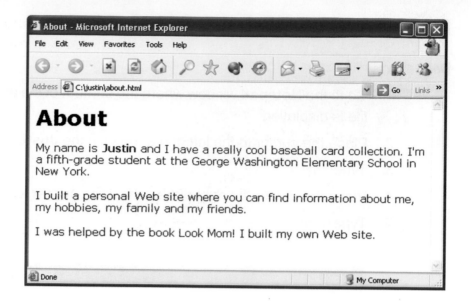

About

My name is **Justin** and I have a really cool baseball card collection. I'm a fifth-grade student at the George Washington Elementary School in New York.

I built a personal Web site where you can find information about me, my hobbies, my family and my friends.

I was helped by the book Look Mom! I built my own Web site.

Figure 3.6: The text *Justin* appears in bold.

The text that appears between the <b> and </b> tags appears in **bold** (as shown in figure 3.6).

Other formats examples:

1. Format the following in bold:

   ◎ George Washington Elementary School

   ```
   at the <b>George Washington Elementary School</b> in
   New York
   ```

   ◎ Look Mom! I built my own Web site

   ```
   the book <b>Look Mom! I built my own Web site</b>.
   ```

2. Change the heading **About** from <h1> to <h2>.

   ```
   <h2>
   About
   </h2>
   ```

3. Save the changes you made in the **about.html** file.

4. Go to the browser window and click the **Refresh\Reload** button to view the changes that you made in the **about.html** file.

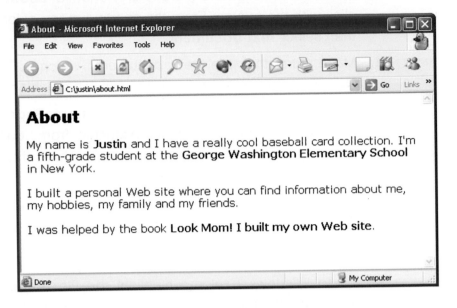

*Figure 3.7: The **about.html** page is even more complete.*

5. Close the browser window displaying the **about.html** file.

6. Close the **Notepad** window displaying the **about.html** file.

Building a new HTML page named homePage.html

1. If Windows Explorer is already open, go to it now. If Windows Explorer is not open, open it before you continue with the following instructions:

   Windows 9x/ME: Click the **Start** button, choose **Programs**, **Windows Explorer**

   Windows 2000/XP: Click the **Start** button, choose **All Programs**, **Windows Explorer**

   Or
   Press ⊞ + **E**.

2. Go to the folder **justin** you created on drive **C**.

3. In the left pane (where there is only one file: **about.html**) right click with the mouse. From the shortcut menu select **New** and then select **Text Document**.

4. Make sure that the new document, which is now called **New Text Document.txt**, is highlighted. If not, highlight it now.

5. Change the name of the document to **homePage.html** (note the change in the file name extension from **.txt** to **.html**). A dialog box will appear asking if you wish to change the file name extension. Click **Yes**.

6. Double click on the file name **homePage.html** (either double or single click depending on your Windows definitions).

Viewing the source code of the HTML page

Return to Windows Explorer, highlight the file **homePage.html,** right-click with the mouse and choose **Open With** and then select **Notepad**. **Notepad** will open, but you will see nothing in it because the file **homePage.html** is still empty.

Typing the content

1. In Notepad, type:

```
<html>
  <head>
    <title>Home Page</title>
    <meta http-equiv="content-type"
      content="text/html;charset=iso-8859-1" />
  </head>
<body>

</body>
</html>
```

2. In the **File** menu, select **Save** to save the file.

3. Type the following text after the <body> tag and before the </body> tag (press **Enter** only where told to do so). You may copy the text from the book's Web site:

   www.bookchamp.net/lookMom.html

   Instructions for using the text are available on the book's Web site under **Help**.

   ```
   Justin's site[Enter]
   I'm Justin and this is the site I built. One day my
   grandfather, who worked for many years as a warehouse
   worker at a big plant, brought me a book: Look Mom! I
   built my own Web site. [Enter]
   The truth is, I was a little disappointed when I saw
   the book. I really wanted a Playstation or a GameBoy
   and I thought: What am I going to do with this book?[Enter]
   So I just droped the book on my desk and I did my
   homework on top of it. One day one of my teachers said
   that she was building a Web site. I thought to myself:
   well, if she can build a Web site, so can I... and this
   is the Web site that I built, with the help of the
   book, of course. [Enter]
   ```

Formating the heading

Format the text "Justin's site" as heading level 2 (<h2>).

```
<h2>Justin's site</h2>
```

Format paragraphs

1. Use the <p> and </p> tags to "surround" each paragraph.

   ```
   <p>
   I'm Justin and this is the site I built. One day my
   grandfather, who worked for many years as a warehouse
   worker at a big plant, brought me a book: Look Mom! I
   built my own Web site.
   </p>
   ```

```
<p>
```
The truth is, I was a little disappointed when I saw the book. I really wanted a Playstation or a GameBoy and I thought: What am I going to do with this book?
```
</p>
<p>
```
So I just droped the book on my desk and I did my homework on top of it. One day one of my teachers said that she was building a Web site. I thought to myself: well, if she can build a Web site, so can I... and this is the Web site that I built, with the help of the book, of course.
```
</p>
```

2. Draw a horizontal line between each paragraph (3 paragraphs, 2 horizontal lines). Look below for the first horizontal line:

```
<p>
```
I'm Justin and this is the site I built. One day my grandfather, who worked for many years as a warehouseman at a big plant, brought me a book: Look Mom! I built my own Web site.
```
</p>
```
→ `<hr />`

The truth is, I was a little disappointed when I saw the book. I really wanted a PlayStation or a GameBoy and I thought: What am I going to do with this book?
```
</p>
```

The `<hr />` tag, which stands for **h**orizontal **r**ule, creates a horizontal line.

3. Change the font of the word "**grandfather**" to a font that is 2 points larger than usual (size="+2"), in olive color (a shade of green) (color="olive").

```
my <font size="+2" color="olive">grandfather</font>,
who...
```

The font size can be selected by using numbers 1 to 7 or by using relative numbers (relative to the font size that precedes it) from -4 up to +4.

Note

Size and color are attributes. An attribute includes three components:

◎   *The name of the attribute, such as "size," "color" etc.*

◎   *The equal sign (=).*

◎   *The value of the attribute, which comes after an equal sign (=) and is placed within quotation marks, such as the value "1" for the attribute "size".*

Note

The use of color will be explained later.

Note

The attribute "size" can have any of the following values: 1, 2, 3, 4, 5, 6 or 7.

The following table shows the values of the "size" attribute as compared with the sizes that are usually used in word processors:

1	2	3	4	5	6	7
8pt	10pt	12pt	14pt	18pt	24pt	36pt

Note

There must be a space before the attribute's name.

4.   Save the changes you made in the **homePage.html** file.

5.   Go to the browser window and click the **Refresh\Reload** button to view the changes that you made in the **homePage.html** file (see figure 3.8).

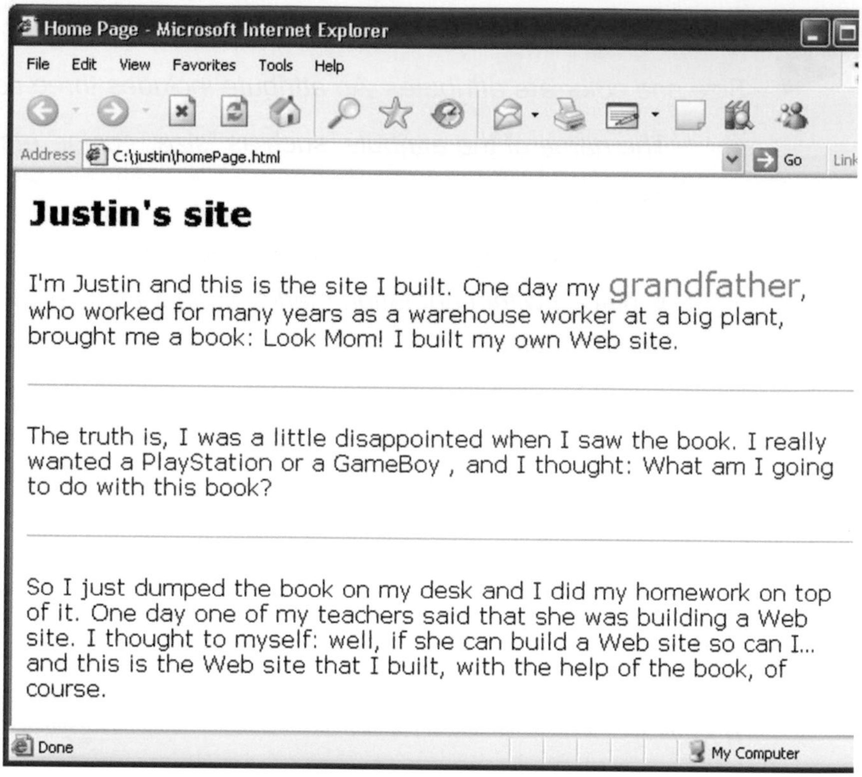

Figure 3.8: *This is how the Home Page (homePage.html) will look.*

Additional formatting exercise

1. Format the word **"grandfather"** in regular font size and change its color to fuchsia (a bright pink, color="fuchsia"). This means you have to delete **size="+2"** from the `<font>` tag and instead of "olive" you have to write "fuchsia", so that it now displays like this:

   ```
   my <font color="fuchsia">grandfather</font>, who...
   ```

2. Save the changes you made in the **homePage.html** file.

3. Go to the browser window and click the **Refresh\Reload** button to view the changes that you made in the **homePage.html** file (see figure 3.9).

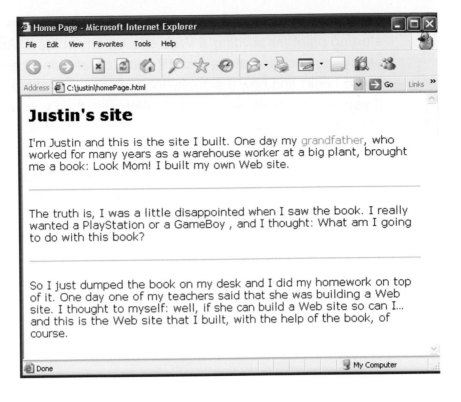

Figure 3.9: This is how the Home Page (homePage.html) will look.

This is so much Fun! Soon you will be able to implement some creative ideas of your own too, but for now… we'll just carry on building Justin's personal Web site. First build a Web site according to the instructions in the book, then later… the sky is the limit!

But if your fingers are simply itching and you really can't wait to build your own Web site about whatever subject you have chosen, then this is my advice:

1. Leave Justin's personal Web site alone and DO NOT touch it!

2. Build your own Web site about your own subject in a separate folder.

You can always use Justin's personal Web site pages as a basic starting point for building a Web site on any subject. And you can always go back and check how it's done (by following the instructions in the book) and how it actually looks (when you use the browser). If you change anything in Justin's Web site, then you will lose track of the book's instructions and you will find it difficult to find your way through the following chapters.

To build your own Web site on any subject (it could be the Los Angeles Dodgers, flowers, your dog – anything you wish), open a new folder. You can refer to the pages that you already built in Justin's Web site for help. You can copy all the files from the **Justin** folder to your new folder for that purpose.

CHAPTER 4

Adding a Link

Linking is the essence of the Web. Links are what make the Web so easy to navigate and use.

With one simple click on a link, the user can move anywhere in your Web site or to any other location on the Internet. Links are what turn the Internet into a worldwide network and you should always remember that this is what visitors to your Web site are looking for.

In this chapter you will:

◎ Add a text link to an image (about.html)

◎ Add a text link to a Web site (about.html)

◎ Build a new Web page (links.html)

◎ Add a text link to a Web site (links.html)

At the end of this chapter your Web pages will look as follows:

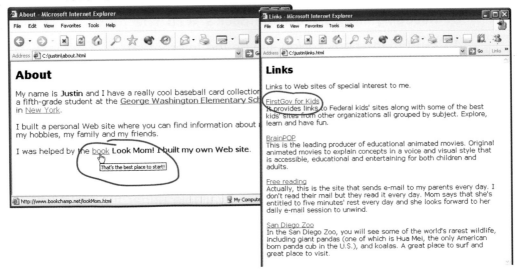

Image please!

Let's begin by creating a text link to an image. First you will need an image for this.

Note

The image can be a photograph, cartoon, logo, etc. An image is a file with an extension like .jpg, .tif, .bmp, .png.

Making a place for images

1. Open Windows Explorer.
2. Go to drive **C**, to the **justin** folder.
3. Create a new folder called **images**, which will be a sub-folder (inside) of the **justin** folder. All the images for your personal Web site will be put into this new **images** folder (justin\images)

The image of George Washington Elementary School, as well as other materials connected with building your personal Web site, are in the book's Web site at:

www.bookchamp.net/lookMom.html, in Chapter 4.

Instructions for using these materials are on the Web site in the **Help** menu.

Downloading images from the book's Web site

4. Surf to the book's Web site on the Internet, at

   www.bookchamp.net/lookMom.html

5. Select **Chapter 4**.
6. In the content pane, on the right hand side, you will see the images: **NYcity.jpg** and **GWES.jpg**
7. Download the two images to your computer. Instructions for downloading the images are available under the **Help** link on the left.

Note

*If you do not find this **C:\justin\images** folder, go back to the paragraph with the title **Making a place for images** and follow the instructions carefully.*

Link a text to an image

Viewing an HTML file in the browser

1. Open Windows Explorer.

2. Go to the folder **justin** you created on drive **C**. The HTML page **about.html** is located in this folder.

3. Double click on the **about.html** file to view it in the browser.

Viewing the source code of the HTML page

Return to Windows Explorer, highlight the file **about.html,** right-click with the mouse and choose **Open With**, and then choose **Notepad**. **Notepad** will open.

Add a text link to an image

You are going to create the text **George Washington Elementary School** a link to the image **GWES.jpg**. Pay attention that the text **George Washington Elementary School** is in bold (you put the `<b>` tag before it and the `</b>` tag after it), so, you are going to make the bolded text a link.

1. Put the cursor before `<b>George` (left of the symbol `<`) and type
   ```
   <a href="images/GWES.jpg" title="A special place to learn">
   ```

2. Now, put the cursor after `School</b>` (right of the symbol `>`) and type

```
</a>
```

The followinf will be displayed:

```
<a href="images/GWES.jpg" title="A special place to
learn"><b>George Washington Elementary School</b></a>
```

The value of the **href** attribute is the resource of the link. In this case, it is an image named **GWES.jpg** in a **images** folder.

The value of the **title** attribute is a toolTip. That's means that when you put the cursor over the link, you will see a small note – that is a toolTip.

Create the text **New York** a link to the image **NYcity.jpg**.

1. Put the cursor before **New York** and type

```
<a href="images/NYcity.jpg" title="The big apple"
target="_blank">
```

2. Now, put the cursor after **New York** and type

```
</a>
```

The following will be displayed:

```
<a href="images/NYcity.jpg" title="The Big Apple"
target="_blank">New York</a>
```

The value **_blank** of the **target** attribute means that when you click on the link, you will see the resource (the address that is written in the **href** attribute) in a new window.

3. Save the changes you made in the **about.html** file (see figure 4.1).

4. Go to the browser window and click the **Refresh\Reload** button to view the changes you made in the **about.html** file.

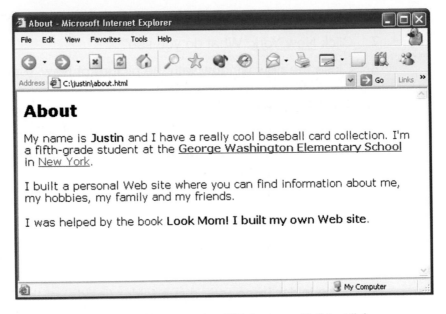

Figure 4.1: The about.html Web page with 2 text links.

5. Click <u>George Washington Elementary School</u>. What do you see?

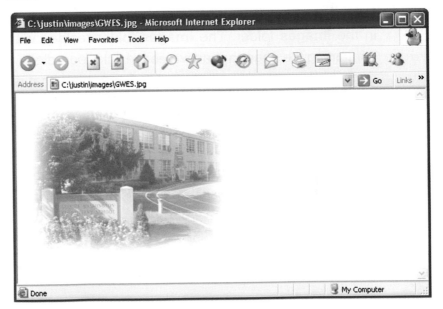

Figure 4.2: The image of George Washington Elementary School (GWES.jpg).

6. Click the browser's Back button.

7. Click <u>New York</u>. What do you see?

8. Close the new window with the picture of New York.

The address of the image is a relative address, because it is relative to the location of the HTML page where the link is activated. You activated the link from the **about.html** page in the **justin** folder on drive **C**, and its address is:

```
C:\justin\about.html
```

The image **GWES.jpg** is located on drive **C** in the **justin** folder, in the sub-folder **images**, and its address is:

```
C:\justin\images\GWES.jpg
```

Since the folder **images** is a sub-folder (inside) of the **justin** folder, which also contains the **about.html** file, you must write the link as follows:

```
<a href="images/GWES.jpg" title="A special place to
learn"><b>George Washington Elementary School</b></a>
```

In fact, this link will work as long as the **GWES.jpg** image is located in the **images** folder. The **images** folder resides within the folder containing the page that activates the link, regardless of the folder's name that could be justin, Alan, Paul or Ashley (that is the meaning of relative address).

Note

Pay attention to the slash symbol. The Windows operating system uses the backslash (\) when displaying file addresses: `images\GWES.jpg`
But on the Internet the forward slash (/) is used: `images/GWES.jpg`

Note

For Windows operating system the backslash (\) and the forward slash (/) are the same when reading file addresses.

The **target** attribute of the <a> tag defines where the content of the link is displayed. If you do not write the **target** attribute, the link will open in the same window. If the value of the **target** attribute is **_blank**, the link will open in a new window.

Link to an Internet address

You are going to create the text **book** a link to this book's Web site.

1. Return to the Notepad window with the content of **about.html** file.

2. Put the cursor before the text **book** (left of the letter b) and type

```
<a href="http://www.bookchamp.net/lookmom.html"
title="That's the best place to start!"
target="_blank">
```

3. Put the cursor after the text **book** (right of the letter k) and type

```
</a>
```

The following will be displayed:

```
<a href="http://www.bookchamp.net/lookmom.html"
title="That's the best place to start!"
target="_blank">book</a>
```

4. Save the changes you made in the **about.html** file.

5. Go to the browser window and click the **Refresh\Reload** button to view the changes you made in the **about.html** file (see figure 4.3).

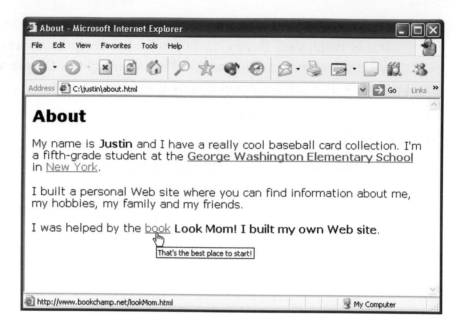

Figure 4.3: Link to an Internet address.

The text **book** is a link. When you put the cursor above (over) the link, you will see a toolTip (title attribute) and the resource (href attribute) in the status bar in the lower left side of the browser window.

Any underlined text on the Internet that appears in <u>blue</u>, <u>red</u> or <u>purple</u> is probably a link.

You can check this out by moving the mouse cursor over the text. If the cursor changes its appearance from ⤢ to 🖑, it confirms that this is a link.

A link is defined by means of the open tag <a> and the end tag </a>. The linked element, in our case this is text, appears between the tags. See the next chapter for how to create an image link.

The value of the attribute **href** of the <a> tag is the address of an HTML page or the address of an image.

Note

Even if you did not denote a particular page on the Web site, but only its name (for example: http://www.bookchamp.net), a page will open. This is the default page as defined in the internet server that stores the Web site that the link is directed to.

6. Close the browser window displaying the **about.html** file.

7. Close the Notepad window displaying the **about.html** file.

Building a new HTML page named links.html

Create a new page with links to your favorite Web sites

1. Open Windows Explorer.

2. Go to **justin** folder on drive **C**.

3. In the right pane, right click with the mouse. From the shortcut menu select **New**, and then **Text Document**.

4. Make sure that the new document, which is now named **New Text Document.txt**, is highlighted. If not, highlight it.

5. Change the name of the new document to **links.html** (note the change in the file name extension name from **.txt** to **.html**). A dialog box will appear asking if you wish to change the file name extension. Click **Yes**.

Viewing an HTML file in the browser

Double click on the **links.html** file (double or single click depending on your Windows definitions). The browser will open, with the file (which is still empty) in it, but nothing will be displayed because the document (**links.html**) is empty.

Viewing the source code of the HTML file

Return to Windows Explorer, highlight the file **links.html,** right-click with the mouse and choose **Open With**, and then choose **Notepad**. **Notepad** will open, but you will see nothing in it because the **links.html** file is still empty.

Typing the structure of a basic HTML page

1. In Notepad type:

```
<html>
  <head>
    <meta http-equiv="content-type"
    content="text/html;charset=iso-8859-1" />
    <title>Links</title>
  </head>
<body>

</body>
</html>
```

2. In the **File** menu, select **Save** to save the file.

Viewing an HTML file in the browser

1. Go to the browser window and click the **Refresh\Reload** button to view the changes you made.

2. On the browser window heading, you will see the word **Links**, which you wrote as part of the `<title>` tag. The content pane will remain empty (white).

Typing the content of the Web page

In Notepad, type the following text after the `<body>` tag and before the `</body>` tag. You can copy the text from the book's Web site at **www.bookchamp.net/lookMom.html**, in Chapter 4.

Instructions for using the text are on the book's Web site under the **Help** menu.

Links`Enter`
Links to Web sites of special interest to me.`Enter`
FirstGov for Kids`Enter`
It provides links to Federal kids' sites along with some of the best kids' sites from other organizations all grouped by subject. Explore, learn and have fun.`Enter`

BrainPOP`Enter`
This is the leading producer of educational animated movies. Original animated movies explain concepts in a voice and visual style that is accessible, educational and entertaining for both children and adults.`Enter`
Free reading`Enter`
Actually, this is the site that sends e-mail to my parents every day. I don't read their mail but they read it every day. Mom says that she's entitled to five minutes' rest every day and she looks forward to her daily e-mail session to unwind.`Enter`
San Diego Zoo`Enter`
In the San Diego Zoo, you will see some of the world's rarest wildlife, including giant pandas (one of which is Hua Mei, the only American born panda cub in the U.S.), and koalas. A great place to surf and great place to visit.`Enter`

Format the heading of the Web page

Format the text "Links" as a heading level 2 (<h2>).
<h2>Links</h2>

Format the paragraphs

1. Use the <p> and </p> tags to surround each paragraph (one paragraph for each Web site) .
   <p>
   Links to Web sites of special interest to me.
   </p>

```
<p>
FirstGov for Kids
It provides links to Federal kids' sites along with
some of the best kids' sites from other organizations
all grouped by subject. Explore, learn and have fun.
</p>
<p>
BrainPOP
This is the leading producer of educational animated
movies. Original animated movies explain concepts in a
voice and visual style that is accessible, educational
and entertaining for both children and adults.
</p>
<p>
Free reading
Actually, this is the site that sends e-mail to my
parents every day. I don't read their mail but they
read it every day. Mom says that she's entitled to five
minutes' rest every day and she looks forward to her
daily e-mail session to unwind.
</p>
<p>
San Diego Zoo
In the San Diego Zoo, you will see some of the world's
rarest wildlife, including giant pandas (one of which
is Hua Mei, the only American born panda cub in the
U.S.), and koalas. A great place to surf and great
place to visit.
</p>
```

2. Save the changes you made in the **links.html** file.

Viewing your HTML file in the browser

1. Go to the browser window and click the **Refresh\Reload** button to view the changes you made in the **links.html** file.

2. Return to the Notepad window where the content of the **links.html** file is displayed.

Add a line break

Add a line break tag (
 tag) following the texts: FirstGov for Kids, BrainPOP, Free Reading and San Diego Zoo.

```
FirstGov for Kids<br />
BrainPOP<br />
Free reading<br />
San Diego Zoo<br />
```

The <br /> tag denotes a line break. When the browser sees a <br /> tag it automatically moves to a new line. In effect, the <br /> tag says: "The following element (text, image) will start from the left". In order to force the browser to start a new line where you want, you must use the <br /> tag.

Format the header to be a link

Each paragraph has a header: FirstGov for Kids for the 1st, BrainPOP for the 2nd and so on.

You are going to create each header a link to a Web site.

Use the <a> tag and its attributes (href, title and target) to create the link.

1. Create the text **FirstGov for Kids** a link to **http://www.kids.gov**, to be opened in a new window with a toolTip saying: "Explore, learn and have fun".

   The following will be displayed:
   ```
   <a href="http://www.kids.gov" title="Explore, learn and
   have fun" target="_blank">FirstGov for Kids</a><br />
   ```

2. Create the text **BrainPOP** as a link to
   http://www.brainpop.com, to be opened in a new window with
   a toolTip saying: "The more you know".

   The following will be displayed:
   ```
   <a href="http://www.brainpop.com" title="The more you
   know" target="_blank">BrainPOP</a><br />
   ```

3. Create the text **Free reading** as a link to
   http://www.dearreader.com
   with a toolTip saying: "Take about 5 minutes to read".

   The following will be displayed:
   ```
   <a href="http://www.dearreader.com" title="Take about 5
   minutes to read">Free reading</a><br />
   ```

4. Create the text **San Diego Zoo** as a link to
    http://www.sandiegozoo.com, to be opened in a new window
    with a toolTip saying: "special Zoo activities".

    The following will be displayed:

    ```
    <a href="http://www.sandiegozoo.com" title="special Zoo
    activities" target="_blank">San Diego Zoo</a><br />
    ```

Now take a look at the source code of the page that you built:

```
<h2>Links</h2>
<p>
Links to Web sites of special interest to me.
</p>
<p>
<a href="http://www.kids.gov" title="Explore, learn and
have fun" target="_blank">FirstGov for Kids</a><br />
It provides links to Federal kids' sites along with
some of the best kids' sites from other organizations
all grouped by subject. Explore, learn and have fun.
</p>
<p>
<a href="http://www.brainpop.com" title="The more you
know" target="_blank">BrainPOP</a><br />
  ::
  ::
<a href="http://www.dearreader.com" title="Take about 5
minutes to read">Free reading</a><br />
  ::
  ::
<a href="http://www.sandiegozoo.com" title="special Zoo
activities" target="_blank">San Diego Zoo</a><br />
```

5. Save the changes you made in the **links.html** file.

View an HTML file in the browser

1. Go to the browser window and click the **Refresh\Reload** button to view the changes you made in the **links.html** file (see figure 4.4).

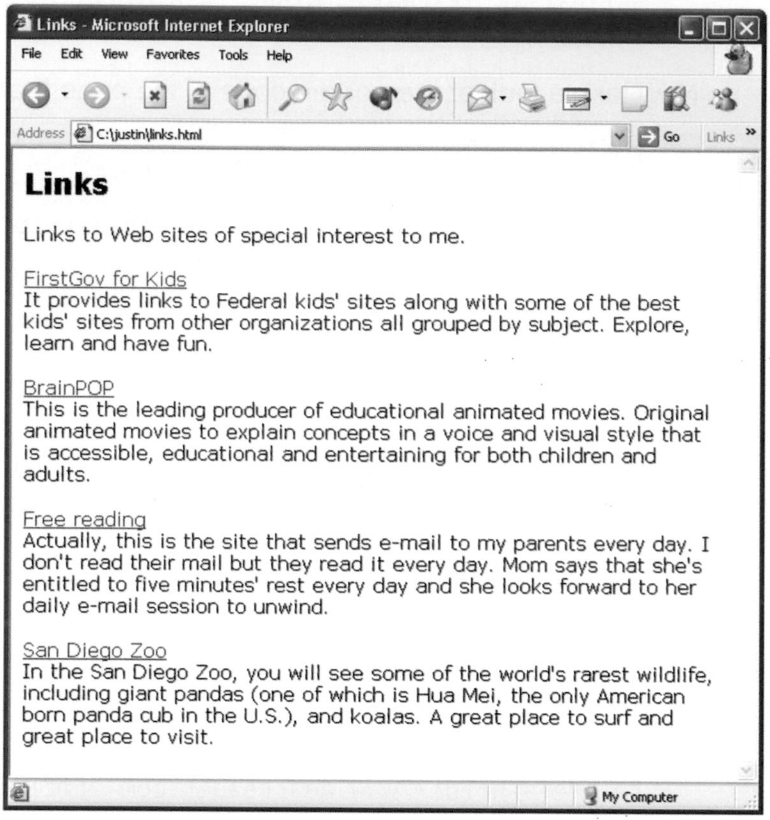

Figure 4.4: The about.html file with links.

2. Close the browser window where the **links.html** file is displayed.

3. Close the Notepad window where the **links.html** file is displayed.

CHAPTER 5

Adding an Image

"An image is worth a thousand words".

You can build your Web pages without images, but, hey, when was the last time you saw any kind of content without images?

Add some images to spice up your Web pages.

In this chapter you will:

◎ Add an image (homePage.html, about.html)

◎ Create an image link to another image (about.html)

At the end of this chapter your Web pages will look as follows:

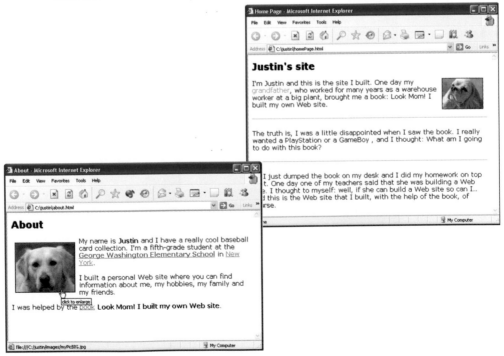

The entire material needed for building a personal Web site is in the book's Web site: **www.bookchamp.net/lookMom.html**. Each chapter has a link on the left of the page (see figure 5.1).

Downloading images from the book's Web site

1. Surf to the book's Web site at

   www.bookchamp.net/lookMom.html

2. Click on Chapter 5 in the menu on the left hand side.

3. In the content pane, on the right side, you will see the images: **grandfather.jpg**, **myPicSmall.jpg**, **myPicBIG.jpg**

4. Download the three images to your computer. Instructions for downloading the images are available under **Help** on the left.

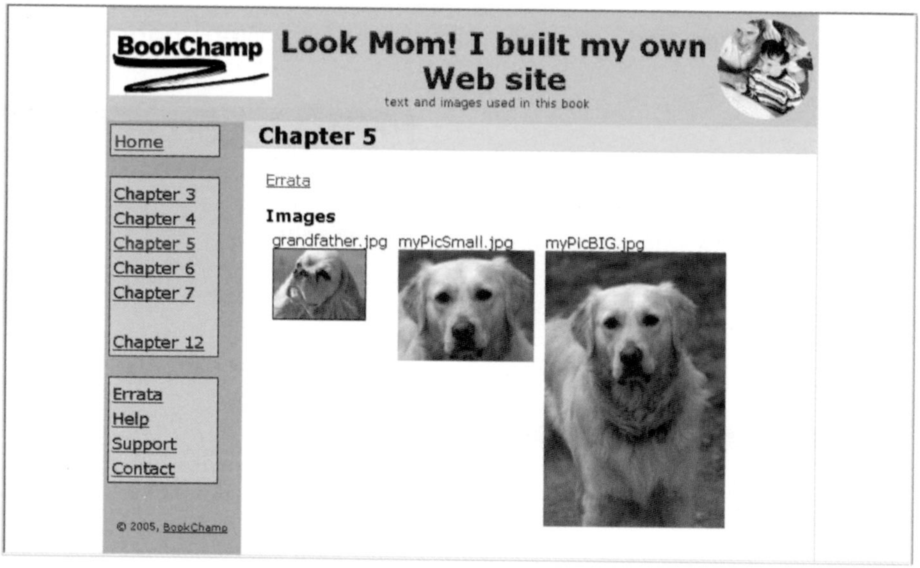

Figure 5.1: The book's Web site.

Add an image to homePage.html

Add the image **images\grandfather.jpg** to the **homePage.html** file, after the line **Justin's site**.

1. Open Windows Explorer.

2. Go to drive **C**, select the **justin** folder that contains the **homePage.html** file that you built.

3. Double click on the **homePage.html** file.

Viewing the source code of the HTML page

Return to Windows Explorer, highlight the file **homePage.html,** right-click with the mouse and choose **Open With**, and then choose **Notepad**.

Typing the content

1. In Notepad, position the cursor following the `</h2>` tag and press **Enter**.

2. Add an image aligned to the right of the window (`align="right"`) with the caption (toolTip, attribute: `title`) **my grandfather**, and with space around it (for vertical space [top, bottom] use the attribute `vspace`, and for horizontal space [left, right] use the attribute `hspace`) in the following manner:
   ```
   <img src="images/grandfather.jpg" align="right"
   hspace="10" vspace="10" title="my grandfather" />
   ```

3. Save the changes that you made in the **homePage.html** file.

4. Go to the browser window and click the **Refresh\Reload** button to view the changes you made in the **homePage.html** file (see figure 5.2).

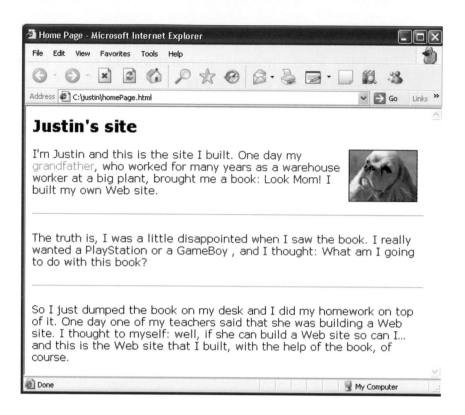

Figure 5.2: *The home page with an image.*

The purpose of the `<img />` tag is to add an image to an HTML page. The value of the **src** attribute is the address of an image.

The image is aligned to the right of the window (align="right"), with a toolTip bearing the words **my grandfather** (attribute: title), and with space around it (vspace="10", hspace="10").

What are the dimensions of the image?

1. To check the dimentions of an image, position the cursor on the image.

2. Right click and from the shortcut menu (also called pop-up menu) select **Properties**.

3. Write the dimensions of the image: _____ x _____ pixels.

4. Close the **Properties** window.

5. Close the browser window where the **homePage.html** file is displayed.

6. Close the Notepad where the **homePage.html** file is displayed.

Add an image to about.html

Add the image **images\myPicSmall.jpg** to the **about.html** file, following the line **About**.

1. Open Windows Explorer.

2. Go to drive **C**, select **justin** folder that contains the **about.html** that you built.

3. Double click on the **about.html** file to view it with the browser.

Viewing the source code of the HTML page

Return to Windows Explorer, highlight the file **about.html,** right-click with the mouse and choose **Open With**, and then choose **Notepad**.

Typing the content

1. In Notepad, position the cursor following the </h2> tag, and press **Enter**.

2. Add the image **images\myPicSmall.jpg** so that it is displayed on the left with space around it.
   ```
   <img src="images/myPicSmall.jpg" align="left"
   vspace="12" hspace="9" />
   ```

3. Save the changes you made in the **about.html** file.

4. Go to the browser window and click the **Refresh\Reload** button to view the changes you made in the **about.html** file (see figure 5.3).

Figure 5.3: The About Web page with an image.

Look at the image. Is the image a link? Yes / No (circle the right answer). Right now, the image is NOT a link. Now we will learn how to link an image.

Link an image to an image

1. Link the image named **myPicSmall.jpg** to the image **images\myPicBIG.jpg** so that it will open in the same window. Create a link with the title (toolTip): **click to enlarge** :

```
<a href="images/myPicBIG.jpg" title="click to enlarge">
 <img src="images/myPicSmall.jpg" align="left"
  vspace="12" hspace="9" />
</a>
```

2. Save the changes you made in the **about.html** file.

3. Go to the browser window and click the **Refresh\Reload** button to view the changes you made in the **about.html** file (see figure 5.4).

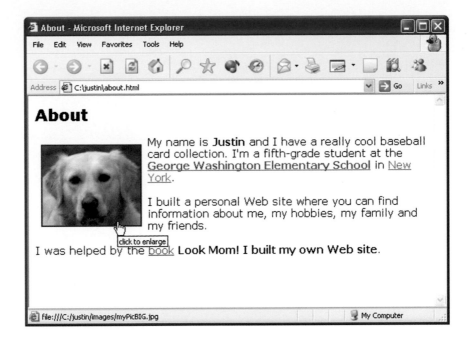

Figure 5.4: *The image is a link.*

4. Click the image to activate the image link.

Now you are looking at a much bigger image of Justin. Can you see his legs? Yes / No (circle the right answer). Of course you can!

5. Close the browser window where the **about.html** file is displayed.

6. Close the Notepad window where the **about.html** file is displayed.

Playing with Color

Color plays a very important role in designing an HTML page. It makes items stand out and divides the page into different sections. It creates the look and feel of the Web site and provides an opportunity for you to show off your creativity.

In this chapter you will:

◎ Change the background color of a Web page

◎ Change the color of a text

At the end of this chapter your Web pages will look as follows:

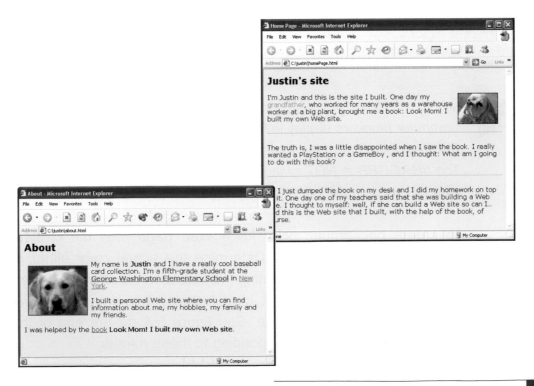

Background color of a Web page – homePage.html file

To add background color to the **homePage.html** Web page, do the following:

1. Open Windows Explorer.

2. Go to drive **C**, select **justin** folder where the **homePage.html** file is located.

3. Double click the **homePage.html** file to view it on the browser.

Viewing the source code of the HTML page

Return to Windows Explorer, highlight the file **about.html,** right-click with the mouse and choose **Open With**, and then choose **Notepad**.

Typing the content

1. In Notepad, position the cursor on the <body> tag between the letter **y** and the symbol **>**.

2. Change the background color of the **homePage.html** to a yellow-orange color, whose RGB is #FBE995.

   ```
   <body bgcolor="#FBE995">
   ```

Note

Computer monitors display in RGB mode:
R = Red, G = Green, B = Blue.
The #RRGGBB is NOT case sensitive, so you can write #FBE995 or #fbe995 and even #FbE995.

To create background color for a Web page, use the `bgcolor` attribute of the <body> tag. Determine the actual color either by denoting the RGB or by denoting the actual name of the color: red, silver, olive, navy, aqua, black, blue, fuchsia, gray, green, teal, lime, purple, yellow, maroon, white. See figure 6.4 (at the end of this chapter) for the colors corresponding to these names.

Font color of a text

1. Change the color of the heading: **Justin's site** to navy.

   ```
   <h2><font color="navy">Justin's site</font></h2>
   ```

2. Save the changes you made in the **homePage.html** file.

3. Go to the browser window and click the **Refresh\Reload** button to view the changes you made in the **homePage.html** file.

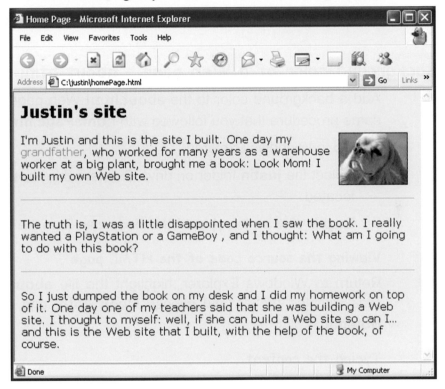

Figure 6.1: *The Home page with background color.*

4. Go to the Notepad window containing the **homePage.html** content.

5. In the **homePage.html** file, change the color of the word "grandfather" into teal (a color between green and cyan).

   ```
   <font color="teal">grandfather</font>
   ```

6. Format the word **grandfather** in bold:
   ```
   <font color="teal"><b>grandfather</b></font>
   ```

7. Save the changes you made in the **homePage.html** file.

8. Go to the browser window and click the **Refresh\Reload** button to view the changes you made in the **homePage.html** file.

9. Close the browser window displaying the **homePage.html** file.

10. Close the Notepad window displaying the **homePage.html** file.

Background color of a Web page – about.html file

Add a background color to the **about.html** Web page. This is the same procedure that you followed with **homePage.html** file.

1. Go to Windows Explorer.

2. Select the **justin** folder on drive **C** where the **about.html** file is located.

3. Double click on the **about.html** file to view it on the browser.

Viewing the source code of the HTML page

Return to Windows Explorer, highlight the file **about.html,** right-click with the mouse and choose **Open With**, and then choose **Notepad**.

Typing the content

1. In Notepad, place the cursor on the `<body>` tag.

2. Change the background color of the **homePage.html** to a yellow-orange color, whose RGB is #FBE995.
   ```
   <body bgcolor="#FBE995">
   ```

Font color of a text

1. Change the color of the heading (the text: **About**) to navy.
   ```
   <h2>
   <font color="navy">About</font>
   </h2>
   ```

2. Save the changes you made in the **about.html** file.

3. Go to the browser window and click the **Refresh\Reload** button to view the changes you made in the **about.html** file (see figure 6.2).

Figure 6.2: The About Web page with background color.

4. Close the browser window displaying the **about.html** file.

5. Close the Notepad window displaying the **about.html** file.

Background color of a Web page - links.html file

Add a background color to the **links.html** Web page. This is the same procedure that you followed with **homePage.html** file.

1. Go to Windows Explorer.

2. Go to drive **C** and navigate to the **justin** folder where the HTML file you built, by the name of **links.html,** is located.

3. Double click on the **links.html** file to view it on the browser.

Viewing the source code of the HTML page

Return to Windows Explorer, highlight the file **links.html,** right-click with the mouse and choose **Open With**, and then choose **Notepad**.

Typing the content

1. In Notepad, position the cursor on the `<body>` tag.

2. Change the background color of the **links.html** Web page to a yellow-orange color, whose RGB is #FBE995.
   ```
   <body bgcolor="#FBE995">
   ```

Font color of a text

1. Change the color of the heading, the text: **Links**, to navy.
   ```
   <h2>
   <font color="navy">Links</font>
   </h2>
   ```

2. Save the changes you made in the **links.html** file.

3. Go to the browser window and click the **Refresh\Reload** button to view the changes you made in the **links.html** file.

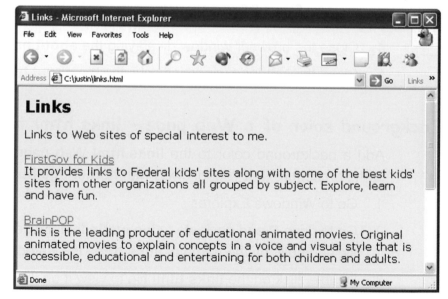

Figure 6.3: The Links Web page with background color.

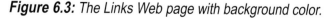

4. Close the browser window displaying the **links.html** file.

5. Close the Notepad window displaying the **links.html** file.

black	silver	gray	white	maroon	red	purple	fuchsia
green	lime	olive	yellow	navy	blue	teal	aqua

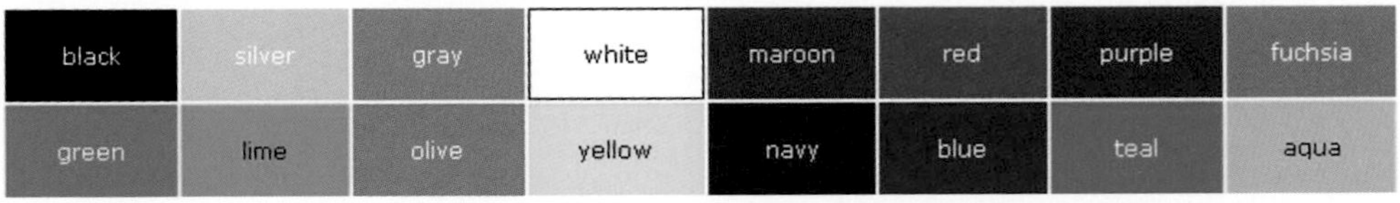

Figure 6.4: *Color names used in HTML.*

Using a Table

Tables are a way of displaying different types of data conveniently and neatly so that they are easy to read. Tables play an important role in formatting data and designing the entire page.

In this chapter you will:

◎ Create a new page named **books.html** containing a table of books that you recommend.

◎ Create a new page named **friends.html** containing a table of your friends.

A table consists of horizontal row(s) and vertical column(s). A cell in the table is created where a row and a column cross each other.

At the end of this chapter your Web pages will look as follows:

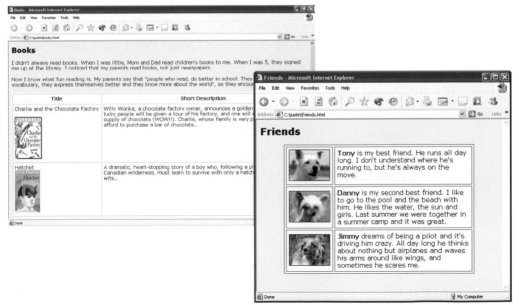

Create a new HTML page – books.html file

The page will be about books that you have read and recommend, and it will be named **books.html**.

1. Open Windows Explorer.

2. Go to the **justin** folder.

3. In the right pane (where you see your HTML files) right click with the mouse. Select **New** from the shortcut menu, then select **Text Document**.

4. Make sure that the new document, which is now called **New Text Document.txt**, is highlighted. If it is not highlighted, highlight the file you created named **New Text Document.txt**.

5. Change the name of the document to **books.html** (pay attention to the change in the file name extension from **txt** to **html**). A dialog box will open asking whether you wish to change the file name extension. Click **Yes**.

6. Double click on the file name **books.html** (double or single click depending on your Windows definitions). The browser will open with the file (which is still empty) inside it, but you will see nothing because the **books.html** file is still empty.

7. Return to Windows Explorer, highlight the file **books.html,** right-click with the mouse and choose **Open With**, and then choose **Notepad**.

8. In Notepad, type:

```
<html>
  <head>
    <meta http-equiv="content-type"
    content="text/html;charset=iso=8859-1" />
    <title>Books</title>
  </head>
<body>

</body>
</html>
```

9. From the Notepad menu bar, select **File** and then select **Save** to save the file.

Adding the text

1. Type the following text after the `<body>` tag and before the `</body>` tag. You can copy the text, from the book's Web site at:
   www.bookchamp.net/lookMom.html
   Instructions can be found under the heading **Help**:

   Books`Enter`
   I didn't always read books. When I was little, Mom and Dad read children's books to me. When I was 5, they signed me up at the library. I noticed that my parents read books, not just newspapers.`Enter`
   Now I know what fun reading is. My parents say that "people who read, do better in school. They have a better vocabulary, they express themselves better and they know more about the world", so they encourage me to read.`Enter`

2. Save the changes you made in the **books.html** file.

3. Go to the browser window and click the **Refresh\Reload** button to view the changes you made in the **books.html** file.

4. Go back to the Notepad window containing the content of the **books.html** file.

5. Change the background color of the Web page to #FBE995.
   `<body bgcolor="#FBE995">`

6. Format the text **Books** to be a heading (h2) with a navy color.
   `<h2><font color="navy">Books</font></h2>`

7. Format the two paragraphs using the `<p>` tag, as follows:
   ```
   <p>
   I didn't always read books. When I was little, Mom and
   Dad read children's books to me. When I was 5, they
   signed me up at the library. I noticed that my parents
   read books, not just newspapers.
   </p>
   ```

```
<p>
Now I know what fun reading is. My parents say that
"people who read, do better in school. They have a
better vocabulary, they express themselves better and
they know more about the world", so they encourage me
to read.
</p>
```

8. Save the changes in the **books.html** file.

9. Go to the browser window, click the **Refresh\Reload** button to view the changes you made in the **books.html** file.

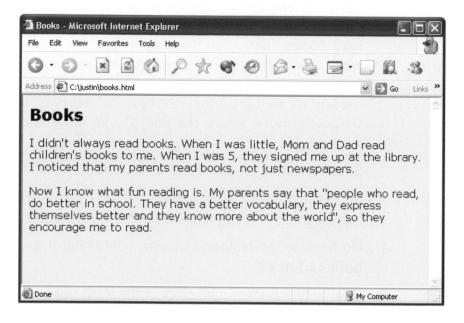

Figure 7.1: The first two paragraphs.

10. Go back to the Notepad window containing the content of the **books.html** file.

Stop! Do not try to create a table yet. Read the rest of this section. The instructions for creating a table will be provided in the next section (soon).

You can copy the text from the book's Web site at: **www.bookchamp.net/lookMom.html**. From the menu on the left-hand side, select Chapter 7. The instructions for using the text are on the Web site under the heading **Help**.

This is the table that you are going to create:

Title	Short Description
Charlie and the Chocolate Factory	Willy Wonka, a chocolate factory owner, announces a golden ticket contest. Five lucky people will be given a tour of his factory, and one will even win a lifetime supply of chocolate (WOW!!). Charlie, whose family is very poor and can hardly afford to purchase a bar of chocolate...
Hatchet	A dramatic, heart-stopping story of a boy who, following a plane crash in the Canadian wilderness, must learn to survive with only a hatchet and his own wits...
The Polar Express	On Christmas Eve, a boy boards a train called "The Polar Express", that is bound for the North Pole. When the train reaches the North Pole, Santa chooses one of the children on board to receive the first gift of Christmas. He chooses the boy, who asks for...

Create a table

In the following section you will create from scratch a table displayed above. Place the cursor following the </p> tag at the end of the second paragraph (ends with "to read."). Press **Enter** and type:

```
<table align="center" border="1" cellpadding="6"
cellspacing="2">
</table>
```

A table begins with the <table> tag and ends with </table> tag. All other tags used when creating a table are included between these tags.

The easiest way to think of a table is as a collection of individual cells arranged in rows and columns. A cell is created where the columns and rows cross each other.

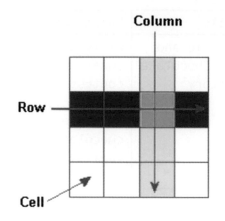

The **align** attribute determines how the table is aligned (horizontal alignment). The **center** value makes sure that it will be positioned in the center of the window (lefr-right).

The **border** attribute determines the boundaries of the table. The default setting is 0 – without any border line.

The **cellpadding** attribute determines the space between the cell border and the text inside the cell.

The **cellspacing** value determines the space between each of the individual cells in the table.

Creating the first row of the table

Place the cursor following the `<table>` tag, press **Enter** and type:
```
<tr>
</tr>
```

The table is built according to rows, therefore you have to create a row before you can create a cell(s) in that row.

Creating cells in the first row

1. Place the cursor following the `<tr>` tag, press **Enter** and type:

```
<td>
 Title
</td>

<td>
 Short description
</td>
```

The following screen displays:

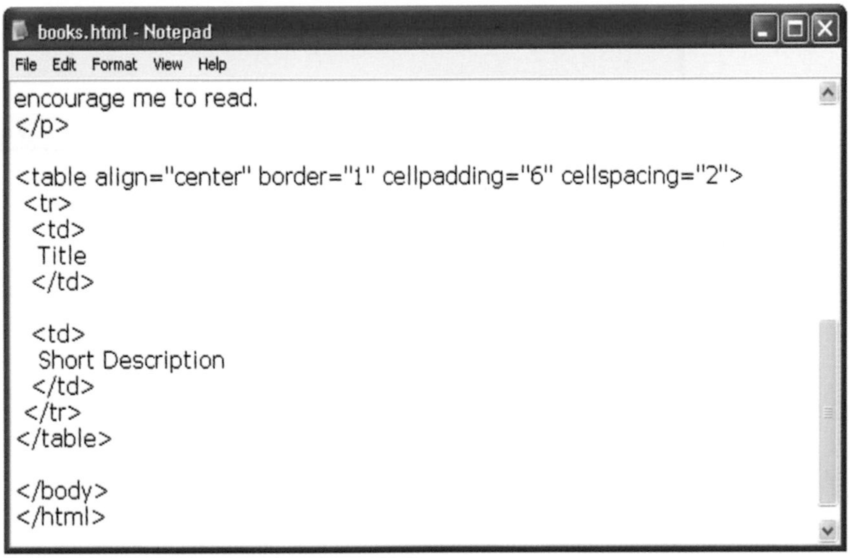

```
books.html - Notepad
File   Edit   Format   View   Help

encourage me to read.
</p>

<table align="center" border="1" cellpadding="6" cellspacing="2">
 <tr>
  <td>
   Title
  </td>

  <td>
   Short Description
  </td>
 </tr>
</table>

</body>
</html>
```

Figure 7.2: The source code of the table.

So far the table that you have made contains 1 row with 2 cells in it.

2. Save the changes you made in the **books.html** file.

3. Go to the browser window and click the **Refresh\Reload** button to view the changes you made to the **books.html** file (see figure 7.3).

Figure 7.3: The first row of the table.

4. Go back to the Notepad window containing the content of the **books.html** file.

Creating the second row of the table

Place the cursor following the last `</tr>` tag which is before the `</table>` tag, press **Enter** and type:

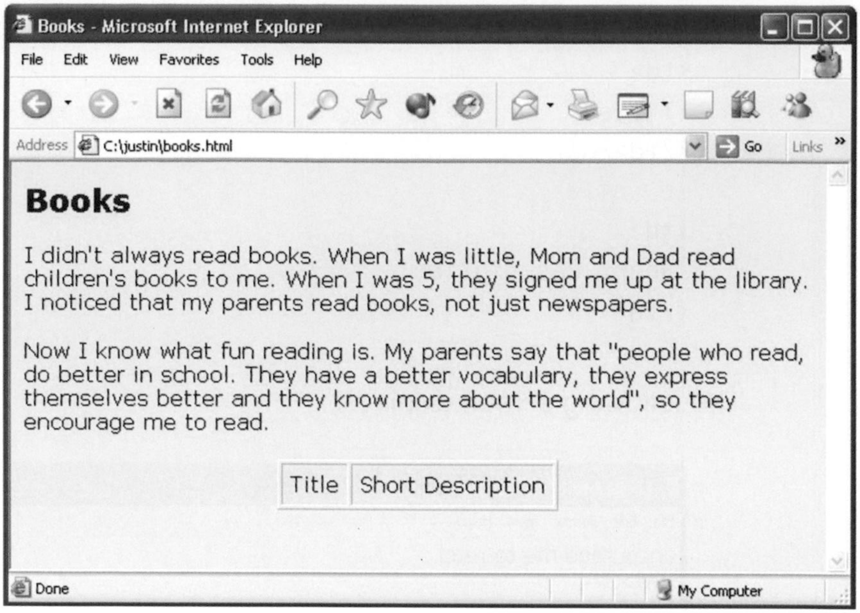

```
<tr>
</tr>
```

Creating cells in the second row

1. Place the cursor following the last `<tr>` tag that you typed, press **Enter** and type:

```
<td>
Charlie and the Chocolate Factory
</td>
```

```
<td>
Willy Wonka, a chocolate factory owner, announces a
golden ticket contest. Five lucky people will be given
a tour of his factory, and one will even win a lifetime
supply of chocolate (WOW!!). Charlie, whose family is
very poor and can hardly afford to purchase a bar of
chocolate...
</td>
```

2. Save the changes you made in the **books.html** file.

3. Go to the browser window and click the **Refresh\Reload** button to view the changes you made to the **books.html** file (see figure 7.4).

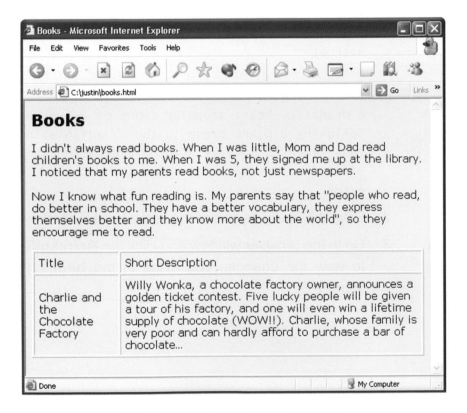

Figure 7.4: The 2 first rows of the table.

4. Go back to the Notepad window containing the content of the **books.html** file.

Creating the third row of the table

1. Place the cursor following the last `</tr>` tag which is before the `</table>` tag, press **Enter** and type:
```
<tr>
</tr>
```

Creating cells in the third row

This procedure is similar to creating the first and second rows.

1. Place the cursor following the last `<tr>` tag that you typed, press **Enter** and type:
```
<td>
Hatchet
</td>
<td>
A dramatic, heart-stopping story of a boy who,
following a plane crash in the Canadian wilderness,
must learn to survive with only a hatchet and his own
wits…
</td>
```

2. Save the changes you made in the **books.html** file.

3. Go to the browser window and click the **Refresh\Reload** button to view the changes you made in the **books.html** file (see figure 7.5).

Figure 7.5: *The table with 3 rows.*

4. Go back to the Notepad window containing the content of the **books.html** file.

Creating the fourth row of the table

Place the cursor following the last `</tr>` tag which is before the `</table>` tag, press **Enter** and type:

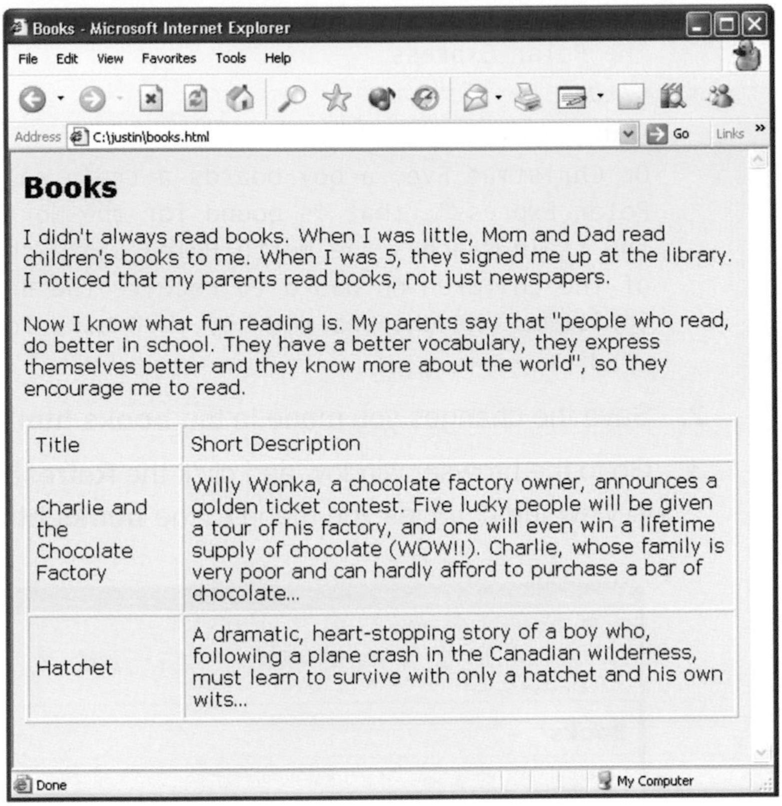

```
<tr>
</tr>
```

Creating cells in the fourth row

1. Place the cursor following the last `<tr>` tag that you typed, press **Enter** and type:

```
<td>
The Polar Express
</td>
<td>
On Christmas Eve, a boy boards a train called "The
Polar Express", that is bound for the North Pole. When
the train reaches the North Pole, Santa chooses one
of the children on board to receive the first gift of
Christmas. He chooses the boy, who asks for...
</td>
```

2. Save the changes you made in the **books.html** file.

3. Go to the browser window and click the **Refresh\Reload** button to view the changes you made to the **books.html** file.

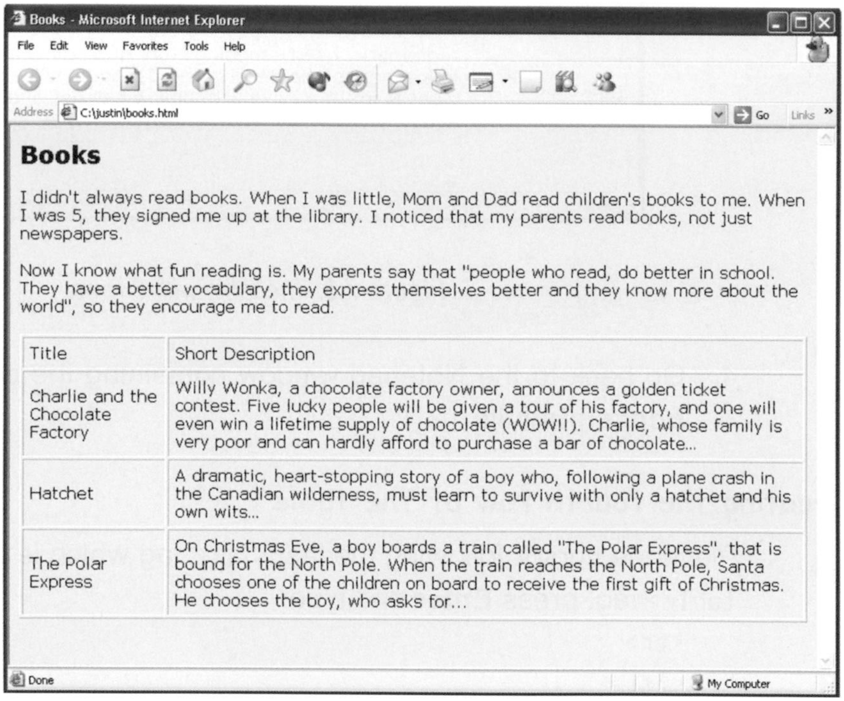

Figure 7.6: The whole table.

4. Go back to the Notepad window containing the content of the **books.html** file.

Tips

Hard white space

The browser determined the width of the columns. You will notice that the title of the book **Charlie and the Chocolate Factory** is written in more than one line. If you would like to display the title in one line (as a single unit, without line breaks), you must allocate **hard white space** by typing ** ** instead of pressing the space bar in the keyboard.

1. Edit the name of the book **Charlie and the Chocolate Factory**. Replace each **space** with ** ** in the text:

    ```
    Charlie and the Chocolate Factory
    The Polar Express
    ```

2. Save the changes you made in the **books.html** file.

3. Go to the browser window and click the **Refresh\Reload** button to view the changes you made to the **books.html** file (see figure 7.7).

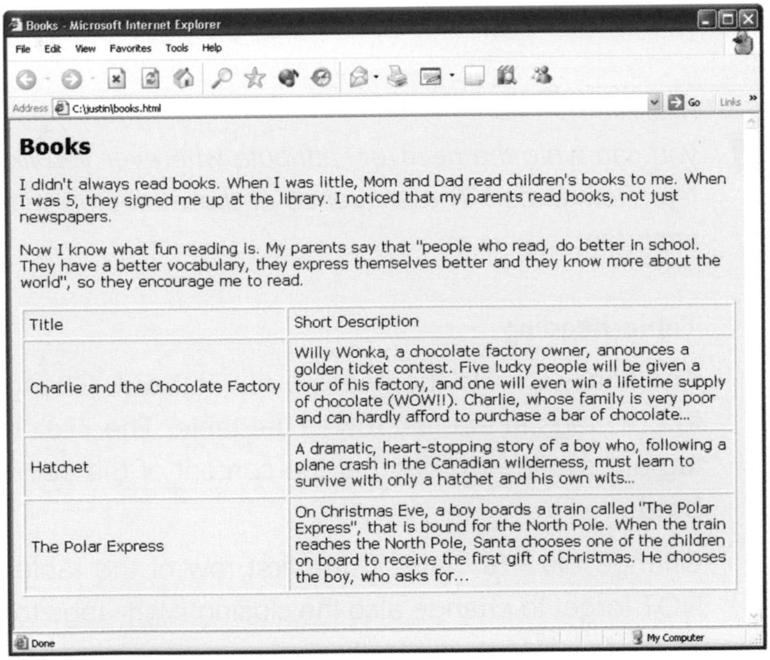

Figure 7.7: *The book titles with hard-white-space.*

Vertical alignment

Now let's align the text in a table cell. The browser's default setting for displaying the content of a table cell is to center it vertically. If you want to align the content to the top of the table cell you must use the `valign` attribute of the `<td>` tag. To align the content of a table cell:

Add the `valign` attribute to the `<td>` tag of the cell which contains the text **Charlie and the Chocolate Factory**.

```
<td valign="top">
```

The same procedure applies to each cell you want to vertically align.

Background color of a table

In order for the table to be seen clearly and not be "over powered" by the background colors of the Web page, let's change the background color of the table to #FEF7D4, by using the **bgcolor** attribute.

Add the `bgcolor` attribute to the `<table>` tag.

```
<table align="center" border="1" cellpadding="6"
cellspacing="2" bgcolor="#FEF7D4">
```

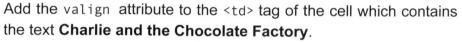

Note

you can write the `bgcolor` attribute wherever you like in the `<table>` tag. Remember! The sequence of the attributes within a tag is NOT important.

Table heading

And finally, create the heading row in **bold**. Change the `<td>` tags to `<th>` tags in the first row of the table. The `<td>` tag and the `<th>` tag are similar, except that the content of the cell is centered and **bold**.

Change the `<td>` tags in the first row of the table to `<th>` and do NOT forget to change also the closing `</td>` tags to `</th>` tags. The changes will look like this:

```
<table align="center" border="1" cellpadding="6"
  cellspacing="2" bgcolor="#FEF7D4">
  <tr>
    <th>
      Title
    </th>
    <th>
      Short Description
    </th>
  </tr>
  <tr>
    <td valign="top">
Charlie and the Chocolate Factory
    </td>
    <td valign="top">
Willy Wonka, a chocolate factory owner, announces a
golden ticket contest. Five lucky people will be given
a tour of his factory, and one will even win a lifetime
supply of chocolate (WOW!!). Charlie, whose family is
very poor and can hardly afford to purchase a bar of
chocolate...
    </td>
  </tr>
  : :
  : :
```

1. Save the changes you made in the **books.html** file.

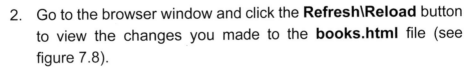

2. Go to the browser window and click the **Refresh\Reload** button to view the changes you made to the **books.html** file (see figure 7.8).

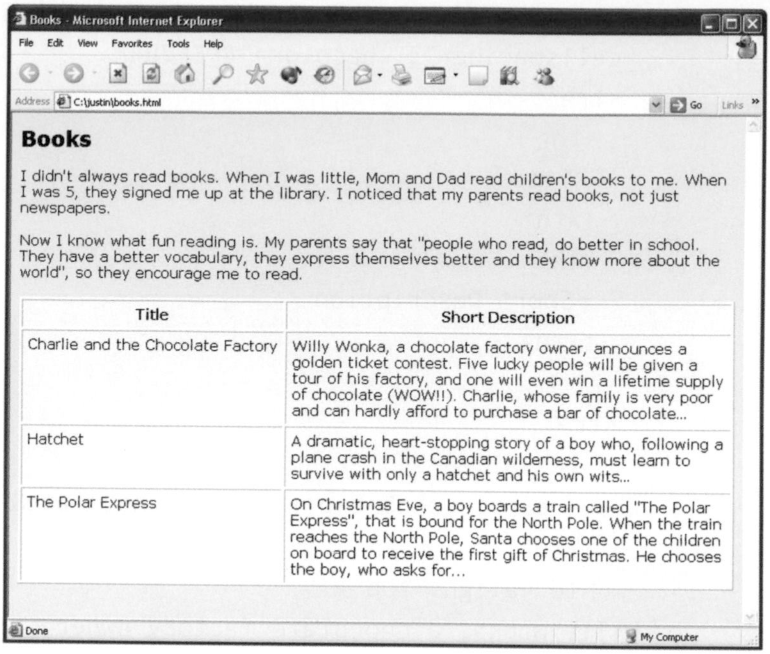

Figure 7.8: Now it is easy to view and read the content of the table.

You are doing fine until now. Let's continue

Add an image to a table

The einther content for building a personal Web site can be found on the book's Web site at **www.bookchamp.net/lookMom.html**. Select Chapter 7 from the menu on the left-hand side.

Downloading images from the book's Web site:

1. Go to the book's Web site at

   www.bookchamp.net/lookMom.html

2. Select Chapter 7 from the menu on the left-hand side.

3. In the content pane, on the right-hand side, you will see the images: **charlie.jpg**, **hatchet.jpg** and **polarExp.jpg**

4. Download the three images to your computer. Instructions for downloading the images are available under **Help** on the left.

Adding an image

Using the `src` and `title` values listed below, add the image of each book beneath the name of the book and in the same cell using the `<img />` tag.

The Book	src	title
Charlie and the Chocolate Factory	images/charlie.jpg	Charlie and the Chocolate Factory by Roald Dahl
Hatchet	images/hatchet.jpg	Hatchet by Gary Paulsen
The Polar Express	images/polarExp.jpg	The Polar Express by Chris Van Allsburg

The following is the code for the three left cells of the table, containing the book title and image:

```
    <td valign="top">
Charlie and the Chocolate Factory
<br /><img src="images/charlie.jpg" title="Charlie and
the Chocolate Factory by Roald Dahl" />
    </td>

    <td valign="top">
Hatchet
<br /><img src="images/hatchet.jpg" title="Hatchet by
Gary Paulsen" />
    </td>

    <td valign="top">
The Polar Express
<br /><img src="images/polarExp.jpg" title="The Polar
Express by Chris Van Allsburg" />
    </td>
```

5. Save the changes you made in the **books.html** file.

6. Go to the browser window and click the **Refresh\Reload** button to view the changes you made to the **books.html** file.

The page will display as follows:

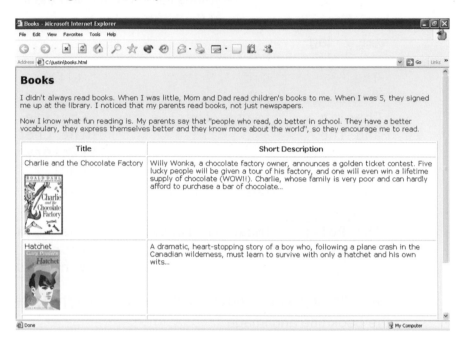

Figure 7.9: The table with images.

1. Close the browser window displaying the **books.html** file.

2. Close the Notepad window displaying the **books.html** file.

Create a new HTML page – friends.html file

Create a new page named **friends.html** with details of your friends.

1. Open Windows Explorer.

2. Go to the **justin** folder.

3. In the right pane (where all your HTML files are) right click. From the shortcut menu select **New** and then select **Text Document**.

4. Make sure that the new document, which is now called **New Text Document.txt**, is highlighted. If not, highlight it.

5. Change the name of the document to **friends.html**. Pay attention to the change in the file name extension from **.txt** to **.html**. A dialog box will open asking whether you wish to change the file name extension. Click **Yes**.

6. Double click on the file name **friends.html** (double or single click depending on your Windows definitions). The browser will open with the file (which is still empty), but you will see nothing because the **friends.html** file is still empty.

7. Return to Windows Explorer, highlight the file **friends.html,** right-click with the mouse and choose **Open With**, and then choose **Notepad**.

8. In Notepad, type:

```
<html>
  <head>
    <meta http-equiv="content-type"
    content="text/html;charset=iso-8859-1" />
    <title>Friends</title>
    </head>
<body>

</body>
</html>
```

9. Change the Web page background color to #FBE995.
```
<body bgcolor="#FBE995">
```

10. Create an header (h2) with the text **Friends** and navy color.
```
<h2><font color="navy">Friends</font></h2>
```

11. From the Notepad menu bar select **File** and then select **Save** to save the file.

Create a table

Stop! Do not try to create a table yet. We are just preparing the background for the next section. For now, just read the rest of this section, then go to the next items and follow the instructions for creating a table. You will create a table of your friends that contains the text below. To save on typing you can copy the text from the book's Web site at **www.bookchamp.net/lookMom.html**. Select Chapter 7 from the menu on the left-hand side. You will find instructions for using the text under the **Help** heading.

> Tony is my best friend. He runs all day long. I don't understand where he's running to, but he's always on the move.
>
> Danny is my second best friend. I like to go to the pool and the beach with him. He likes the water, the sun and girls. Last summer we were together in a summer camp and it was great.
>
> Jimmy dreams of being a pilot and it's driving him crazy. All day long he thinks about nothing but airplanes and waves his arms around like wings, and sometimes he scares me.

Create a table with 3 rows (the same number as the friends), each row with a single cell containing a description of one friend.

Place the cursor following the </h2> tag, press **Enter** and type:

```
<table align="center" border="1" cellpadding="6"
cellspacing="4" bgcolor="#FEF7D4">
</table>
```

Creating the first row of the table

Place the cursor following the `<table>` tag, press **Enter** and type:

```
<tr>
</tr>
```

Creating one cell in the row

1. Place the cursor following the last `<tr>` tag that you typed, press **Enter** and type:

```
<td valign="top">
Tony is my best friend. He runs all day long. I don't
understand where he's running to, but he's always on
the move.
</td>
```

2. Save the changes you made in the **friends.html** file.

3. Go to the browser window and click the **Refresh\Reload** button to view the changes you made in the **friends.html** file.

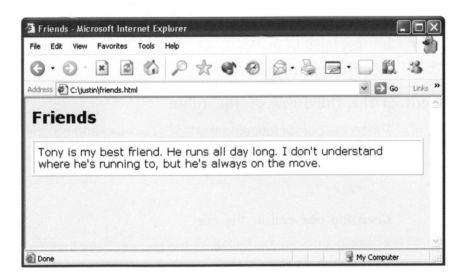

Figure 7.10: The first row of the table.

4. Go back to the Notepad window containing the content of the **friends.html** file.

Creating the next rows will follow the prcedure of the first one.

Creating the second row of the table

Place the cursor following the last `</tr>` tag which is before the `<table>` tag, press **Enter** and type:

```
<tr>
</tr>
```

Creating one cell in the row

1. Place the cursor following the last `<tr>` tag that you typed, press **Enter** and type:

   ```
   <td valign="top">
   ```

   Danny is my second best friend. I like to go to the pool and the beach with him. He likes the water, the sun and girls. Last summer we were together in a summer camp and it was great.

   ```
   </td>
   ```

2. Save the changes you made in the **friends.html** file.

3. Go to the browser window and click the **Refresh\Reload** button to view the changes you made to the **friends.html** file.

4. Go back to the Notepad window containing the content of the **friends.html** file.

Creating the third row of the table

Place the cursor folloeing the last `</tr>` tag and before the `</table>` tag, press **Enter** and type:

```
<tr>
</tr>
```

Creating one cell in the row

1. Place the cursor following the last `<tr>` tag that you typed, press **Enter** and type:

   ```
   <td valign="top">
   ```

   Jimmy dreams of being a pilot and it's driving him crazy. All day long he thinks about nothing but airplanes and waves his arms around like wings, and sometimes he scares me.

   ```
   </td>
   ```

2. Save the changes you made in the **friends.html** file.

3. Go to the browser window and click the **Refresh\Reload** button to view the changes you made in the **friends.html** file.

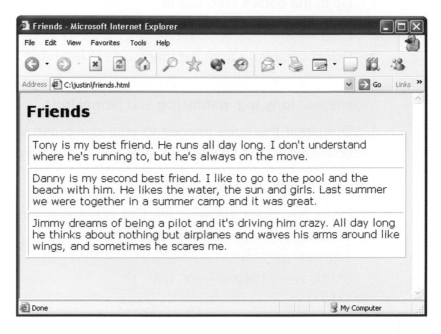

Figure 7.11: The table with 3 rows.

4. Go back to the Notepad window containing the content of the **friends.html** file.

Additional layout designs

Bold the names of your friends: Tony, Danny and Jimmy:

```
<b>Tony</b> is my best friend...
<b>Danny</b> is my second best...
<b>Jimmy</b> dreams of being...
```

Note
You can delete any empty row that were created in the course of making the table.

Add a column to the table

Downloading images from the Web site of the book

1. Go to the book's Web site at

   www.bookchamp.net/lookMom.html

2. Select Chapter 7 from the menu on the left-hand side.

   In the content pane, on the right-hand side, you will see the images: **tony.jpg, danny.jpg** and **jimmy.jpg**

3. Download the three images to your computer. Instructions for downloading the images are available under **Help** on the left.

Add a cell with an image

1. Place the cursor following the first <tr> tag in the **friends.html** Web page and press **Enter** and type.

```
<td valign="top">
 <img src="images/Tony.jpg" />
</td>
```

You created a new cell in the first row of the table. Now there are 2 cells in that row.

2. Place the cursor following the second <tr> tag, press **Enter** and type:

```
<td valign="top">
 <img src="images/Danny.jpg" />
</td>
```

3. Place the cursor following the third <tr> tag, press **Enter** and type:

```
<td valign="top">
 <img src="images/Jimmy.jpg" />
</td>
```

4. Save the changes you made in the **friends.html** file.

5. Go to the browser window and click the **Refresh\Reload** button to view the changes you made to the **friends.html** file.

Figure 7.12: The table after you added a column with images.

6. Go back to the Notepad window containing the content of the **friends.html** file.

Change the width of a table

1. Change the width of the table to 80% of the width of the window displaying the page, center the table, change the border color of the table (attribute: `bordercolor`) to **brown**.

```
<table align="center" border="1" cellpadding="6"
cellspacing="4" width="80%" bgcolor="#FEF7D4"
bordercolor="brown">
```

The **width** attribute determines the width of the table. If you do not set a width for the table, the browser will do it, based on the content of the table.

2. Save the changes you made in the **friends.html** file.

3. Go to the browser window and click the **Refresh\Reload** button to view the changes you made to the **friends.html** file.

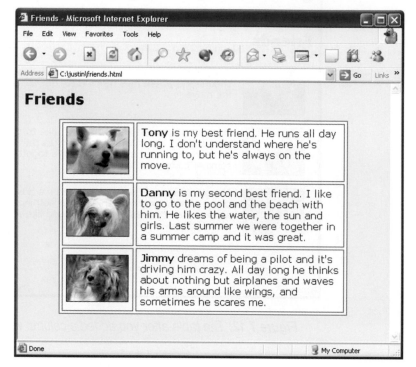

Figure 7.13: The table with a brown border.

4. Close the browser window displaying the **friends.html** file.

5. Close the Notepad window displaying **friends.html** file.

Using a Table for Page Layout

So far your personal Web site contains the following pages: **homePage.html, about.html, books.html, links.html** and **friends. html**. All the pages are displayed at full window width. This is not the most attractive display format. Also, when the pages are printed, the margins will be cut off. It is advisable to have some space between the content of the page and the edges of the window.

In this chapter you will:

◎   Format your page with a table.

The figure below illustrates the **homePage.html** page before the change (as it is now) and following the change, which you are about to make:

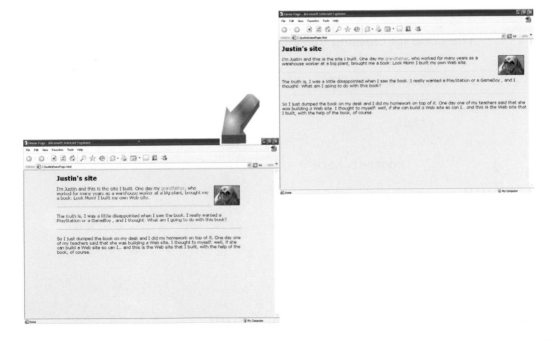

How do you create space between the content of the page and the edge of the window?

You will format the entire page as a table with 1 row and 1 column, but:

◎ The width of the table will be less than 100%.

◎ The table will be in the center of the window (left/right).

So, the outcome of this is that there will be a space between the table and the edge of the window, and that is exactly what we want!

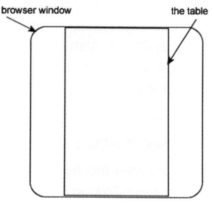

browser window   the table

The content will be inside the column.

The code for creating the table will be as follows:

```
<body...>
<table border="0" width="76%" align="center">
 <tr>
   <td>

       content here

   </td>
 </tr>
</table>
</body>
```

Explanation:

◎ The table consists 1 row and 1 column.

◎ The width of the table is 76% of the browser window's width and it appears in the center (left/right). You can change this % as you wish.

◎ The content of the cell can be anything you want: text, tables, images...

So how do you do this?

1. Open Windows Explorer.

2. Go to drive **C**, navigate to the **justin** folder which contains the **homePage.html** file.

3. Double click on the **homePage.html** file to view it on the browser.

Viewing the source code of the HTML page

Return to Windows Explorer, highlight the file **homePage.html,** right-click with the mouse and choose **Open With**, and then choose **Notepad**.

Building the page layout

1. Place the cursor following the <body> tag, press **Enter** and type:
```
<table border="0" width="76%" align="center">
  <tr>
    <td>
```

2. Press **Ctrl+End** on the keyboard to go to the end of the source code displayed in the Notepad window.

3. Place the cursor before the </body> tag and press **Enter**. Place the cursor at the beginning of the new line that you have just created, and type the following:
```
    </td>
  </tr>
</table>
```

4. Save the changes you made in the **homePage.html** file.

5. Go to the browser window and click the **Refresh\Reload** button to view the changes you made in the **homePage.html** file.

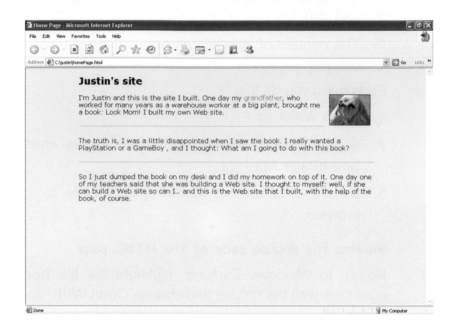

Figure 8.1: The page layout formated with a table.

6. Close the browser window displaying the **homePage.html** file.

7. Close the Notepad window displaying the **homePage.html** file.

You used a table for the **homePage.html** page layout. Now it is time to format the other Web pages to create a uniform page layout for your Web site.

To apply the new layout to all the Web pages that you created, repeat items 1 to 7 for each individual Web page that you made: **about.html, books.html, links.html** and **friends.html**. Make sure that you "wrap" the existing content for each page with table tags. Notice that these changes do not replace any existing tag, you just add tags.

Note

The default value of the border *attribute in the* <table> *tag is 0 (zero), so it is not really necessary to write* border="0" *in the code. If you would like to view the table's border, you can change the value from 0 to 1, view the border, and then when you want to hide the border just place the value with 0 again.*

Creating a Menu and Completing Your Web Site

At this stage, the pages of your Web site are ready. A page stands on its own, independently. In order for it to be a Web site it must have a menu, which is really a navigation mechanism, to connect and link the pages together.

In this chapter you will:

◎ Create a menu for your Web site

◎ Learn how to display the menu on each of the Web pages that you built.

At the end of this chapter your Web pages will look as follows:

A menu

So far you have designed the following pages of your personal Web site: **homePage.html, about.html, books.html, links.html** and **friends.html**. Every page stands alone and the time has now come to place them all into the structure of a complete Web site.

Every Web site has a structure, that can be seen in the menu (toolbar of links) that is located either at the top or on one side (left or right) of the page. The figure below illustrates the structure of a site with the menu at the top as follows:

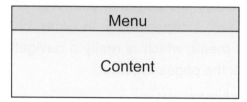

Your menu will contain links to the pages on your site: **homePage. html, about.html, books.html, links.html** and **friends.html**.

You will create a new **HTML** page that will be named **menu.html**. It will contain five links (a link to each Web page you have) and will look like this:

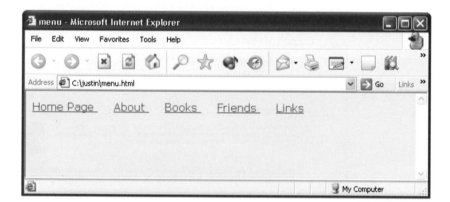

Figure 9.1: The menu.

Creating a menu

Create a new HTML page – menu.html file

Create a new page named **menu.html** with links to your Web pages.

1. Open Windows Explorer.

2. Go to the folder you created named **justin**.

3. In the right pane (where all your HTML files are) right click. From the shortcut menu select **New** and then select **Text Document**.

4. Make sure that the new document, which is now called **New Text Document.txt**, is highlighted. If not, highlight it.

5. Change the name of the document to **menu.html** (pay attention to the change in the file name extension from **.txt** to **.html**). A dialog box will open asking whether you wish to change the file name extension. Click **Yes**.

6. Double click on the **menu.html** file (double or single click depending on your Windows definitions). The browser will open with the file (which is still empty) inside it, but you will see nothing because the **menu.html** file is still empty.

7. Return to Windows Explorer, highlight the file **menu.html,** right-click with the mouse and choose **Open With**, and then choose **Notepad**.

8. In Notepad, type the following:

```html
<html>
   <head>
    <meta http-equiv="content-type"
     content="text/html;charset=iso-8859-1" />
    <title>menu</title>
   </head>
<body bgcolor="#FBE995">
      <a href="homePage.html" title="Home Page for
      Justin's Web site" target="_top">
       Home Page
      </a>   
      <a href="about.html" title="Read more about me"
      target="_top">
       About
      </a>   

      <a href="books.html" title="The books I read"
      target="_top">
       Books
      </a>   

      <a href="friends.html" title="These are my best
      friends" target="_top">
       Friends
      </a>   

      <a href="links.html" title="Links to Web sites of
      special interest to me" target="_top">
       Links
      </a>
   </body>
   </html>
```

9. Save the **menu.html** file in Notepad.

10. Display the **menu.html** file on the browser.

Please note that the value of the `target` attribute of the `<a>` tag must be `_top`. **T**his is essential for what you are going to do next.

Thinking

Click on the **Books** link.

Please notice that the menu disappears and the **books.html** page appears instead of it. That's fine, but it is not possible to navigate your Web site if the menu disappears from the screen.

So I have an idea. Instead of writing a menu page by the name of **menu.html**, I will write the menu (links) on each of the pages of the Web site. A great idea! Yes, that's it – the menu should be part of every single page on your personal Web site.

Let us suppose (don't actually do anything yet, apart from thinking) that every single page on your Web site has links to every other page on the site. What will happen when you add a new page to your Web site? You will still want every other page on the site to have a link to the new page, right? You will have to go into every individual Web page and add the link – that's a lot of detailed work with a good chance of making a mistake somewhere.

So let's think some more (still without doing anything, only thinking). What will happen if one day you decide to change the name of the **books.html** page to **myBooks.html**? Then you would have to go into every individual page on your Web site and change the link from **book.html** to **myBooks.html**. Again, a lot of work with a big chance of making a mistake.

What should you do? Very soon you are going to embed the menu page **menu.html** in every one of the Web pages of your Web site. This means that you will have ONE menu page by the name of **menu.html** (that you have already created), but it will also be a part of every page on your Web site.

Now you are probably thinking: "Wow! That's really cool! Every change I want to create to the menu (**menu.html** Web page) will be made on every other page too! But how will the other pages be updated? "

Embedding HTML pages

You do not copy the menu (the links) onto every one of the pages on your Web site, but instead you "embed" it. There is no menu on every Web page, but there is a kind of "room" or "space" in every page for the menu page (menu.html).

As soon as the browser activates (loads) any page, it "absorbs" the content of the menu page into the activated page and displays it as one page.

Below is an illustration of what will happen:

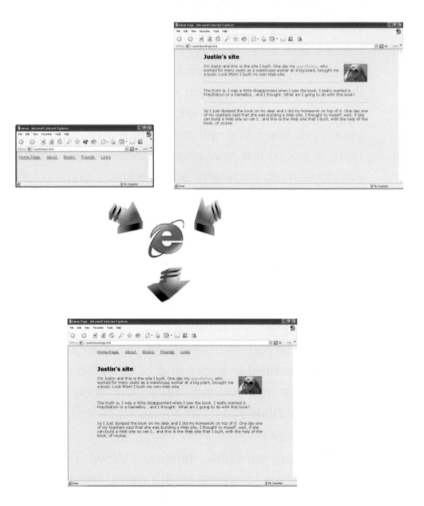

Figure 9.2: Embedding an HTML page in another HTML page.

Embedding an HTML page in another HTML page

1. View the **homePage.html** Web page in the browser.

2. View the source code of the **homePage.html** page in Notepad.

3. Position the cursor before the `<h2>` tag, and press **Enter**. Place the cursor at the beginning of the new line that you created and type the following code:

```
<iframe src="menu.html"
  width="100%" height="50" align="center"
  frameborder="0"
  marginheight="0" marginwidth="0" scrolling="no">
</iframe>
```

4. Save the **homePage.html** Web page.

5. Go to the browser and click **Refresh\Reload** to view the changes you made in the **homePage.html** file (see figure 9.3).

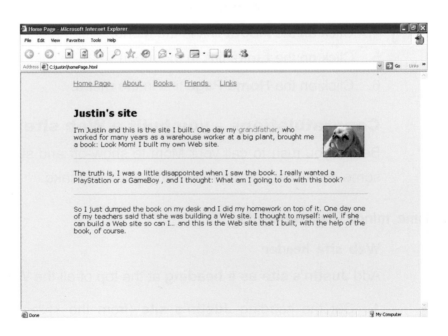

Figure 9.3: *The menu embeded in the Home page.*

6. Close the browser window displaying the **homePage.html** Web page.

7. Close the Notepad window displaying the **homePage.html** content.

Note

You can create a "room" or "space" for the menu.html Web page in any other page by using the <iframe>...</iframe> *tag.*

Applying the menu for each page

Repeat items 1 to 7 for each of the other Web pages you created: **about.html, books.html, friends.html, links.html.**

Verifying your Web site menu

1. View the **homePage.html** file in the browser.

2. Click on the **Books** link in the menu.

3. Click on the **Friends** link in the menu.

4. Click on the **About** link in the menu.

5. Click on the **Links** link in the menu.

6. Click on the **Home Page** link in the menu.

Congratulations – you built a Web site!

Before you rush to call your Mom to show-off and share, here are some additional tiny improvements you can make.

Some minor improvements

Web site header

Add **Justin's site as a heading** at the top of all the Web pages.

1. Cut the heading **Justin's site** (from the <h2> tag to the </h2> tag) from the **homePage.html** page and paste it onto the **menu.html** page immediately following the <body> tag. Save the two Web pages.

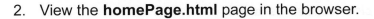

2. View the **homePage.html** page in the browser.

You can see the heading **Justin's site** on the page, but where are the links to the other pages? You can't see the links because there is not enough room (height) on the **homePage.html** page for the **menu.html** page.

To adjust the height of the `<iframe>` tag that contains the menu:

1. View the source code of the **homePage.html** page in Notepad.

2. In the `<iframe>` tag, change the value of the height attribute from 50 to 100 (if 100 is not good enough, you can give it some other value).

3. Go to the browser and click **Refresh\Reload** to view the changes you made in the **homePage.html** page (as shown below).

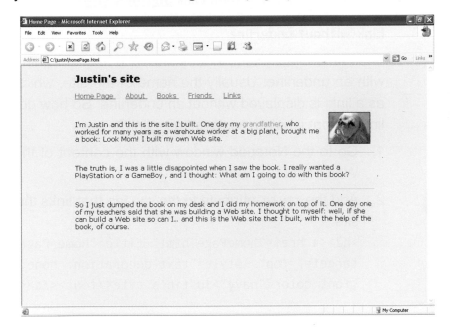

Figure 9.4: *The menu with the header.*

Repeat items 1 to 3 for each of the other pages: **about.html, books.html, friends.html, links.html.**

Web site header as a link

To link the name of the site (**Justin's site**) to the home page:

1. Open the **menu.html** page in the browser.

2. View the source code of the **menu.html** page in Notepad.

3. Link the heading **Justin's site** to the **homePage.html** page as follows:

   ```
   <h2><a href="homePage.html" title="Home Page"
    target="_top"><font color="navy">Justin's site
   </font></a></h2>
   ```

4. Save the **menu.html** document in Notepad.

5. Go to the browser and click on **Refresh\Reload** to view the changes you made.

6. Click <u>Books</u>, and then click **<u>Justin's site</u>**.

Link without underline

The name of the site (**Justin's site**) is a text link. A link is displayed with an underline. Usually the name of the site, which also serves as a link, is displayed without an underline. So how do you create a link without it being displayed as a link?

1. Go to the Notepad window with the content of the **menu.html** Web page.

2. Add the `style` attribute to the `<a>` tag that links the name of the site.

   ```
   <h2><a href="homePage.html" title="Home Page"
   target="_top"  style="text-decoration: none;">
   <font color="navy">Justin's site</font></a></h2>
   ```

Note
Pay attention that the first symbol of the `style` *attribute is : (colon) and the second is ; (semicolon)*

3. Save the **menu.html** document in Notepad.

4. Go to the browser and click **Refresh\Reload** to view the changes you made.

Figure 9.5: *Your Web site is READY!*

5. Close the Notepad window displaying the **menu.html** content.

Now… run and call your Mom!

What Next?

If you have progressed to this chapter then you have already built a **personal Web site**. It's true that it is Justin's site, but it is still a personal Web site. I am sure that you have some creative ideas on what to do with this personal site, as well as creative ideas for making your own Web site.

My advise is:

1. **Do not** touch Justin's personal Web site.
2. Build your own site about any subject you choose in a separate folder.

You can use Justin's personal site as the basis for building another site about any subject. You can always go back and see how any one of the stages was done (according to the instructions in the book) and how it looks in reality (when you activate the Web pages). However, if you change anything in Justin's personal Web site you will lose the connection between the instructions in the book and the completed site, and it will be difficult for you to refer to the book for help later on.

To build your own Web site on any subject of youe choice: LA Dodgers, flowers, your dog…, open a new folder. You can use the pages you already built in Justin's Web site to help you. Just copy some of the files – or all of them if you prefer – from the **justin** folder to the new folder that you just opened. You can find more details in Chapter 11.

But for now, the time has come to put the Justin Web site on the Internet. It's true that this is not the site that you really want to put on the Internet, but for the sake of practice and experience it is a good idea to do this first with Justin's site.

Part II will explain how to put your Web site on the Internet.

If you want to build your Web site, move on to the next chapter.

Building Your Own Web Site

Building an Internet Web site is not only for your own ego. Sharing your special knowledge is a way of contributing to the community. You have an opportunity to create something and show it to the entire community, to express an opinion and present it publicly. Something else you need in order to build an Internet site is courage. Anything you put into the content of your Web site is potentially exposed to millions of surfers all over the world – children and adults, men and women, all races and religions, people with many different views and opinions.

As in many things in life, building a Web site also requires some planning. Planning takes time, you know! I understand just how you feel. I understand that you are eager to see your Web site ready quickly and you are saying: "Let's get on with it. Who needs all that planning? And even if I do need it, why not just do it as I go along…." Many people have thought the same thing and started to push ahead right away, as fast as possible.

Some of the difficulties they encounter are:

The building process got stuck, and not because of insufficient knowledge or inadequate tools

Or

The building was never completed – what seemed to be small, quick and simple at first, turned out to be a long drawn-out, endless process.

One way or another, it didn't come out like they imagined or like they wanted. So why not let other people's experience help you, people who discovered that **NOT** planning the site properly is the main reason for running into problems and difficulties.

Checklist for building your Web site

- ☐ Choose a subject for your Web site.
- ☐ Collect and prepare materials (text, images) on your PC.
- ☐ Design your Web site.
- ☐ Build your own Web site on your PC.
- ☐ Upload your Web site onto the Internet.
- ☐ Maintenance: Add, Update, Delete, Change….

Choosing a subject for your Web site

Here is some advice to help you decide mainly what **NOT** to publish on your own site:

- ◎ Never display any content (images or text) that you would not be willing to show your Mom. Choose content (images and text) that you would be proud to have your mother see.

- ◎ Never display any content (images or text) that you would not be willing to talk about in school or at your local youth club. Make sure you can talk openly about the content with your friends.

- ◎ Never display any content that could be considered as libel, slander or defamation (if you do not know the meaning of the last three words... ask your parents).

Also…

◎ You must be aware of any copyrights regarding material that you use on your Web site. Even if you are under 18 years old and/or are not familiar with the law, that does not give you the right to disregard copyrights.

◎ The content should be legal and in keeping with the spirit of the law, otherwise you could end up being flooded with legal claims that could land you and/or your parents in serious trouble for the rest of your lives and could even leave you completely broke.

Apart from this, the Internet is a free and open environment where you can publish anything that comes to your mind: text, images, video clips and audio clips that you made yourself and anything else that can be produced on digital media.

The subject and content of a Web site are more important than the "packaging" (the way it looks visually). Refer to the summary at the end of the chapter for information on what keeps users coming back to your site. A site with no subject and no content is meaningless. That would be like making a really attractive dust jacket for a book that contains only empty pages. Even if someone were to pick up the book in a bookshop and flick through it because the cover caught the eye, it's doubtful whether anyone would want to buy it and take it home. An attractive Web site without content may impress people who see the home page, but once they go into the other pages they will only be disappointed, and of course no one will want to surf in that site again.

A **good Web site** is one that surfers find interesting and that they will want to make return visits to. A site does not have to include every subject under the sun. It can concentrate on a single, very narrow and specific subject and still attract surfers to return to it. Let's say, a site about cultivating a particular species of rare flower. It is obvious that not every surfer on the Web will be interested in exactly that flower, but the site will appeal to anyone who is especially interested in the subject of gardening and growing flowers, or to surfers who need information about a particular flower (such as students).

Those people will be very pleased to find a site like this, since the chances are that Web sites about that flower are quite rare, as rare as the flower itself. So maybe that site will not be visited by a million surfers, but no one can claim that it is not entitled to a place on the Internet, or that it does not fulfill the purpose it was created for, or that surfers who visit it find nothing of interest there.

Making a good personal Web site poses a serious challenge. A **personal Web site** is usually one where the site owner tells us about his life, his hobbies and anything else he does or is interested in. But a site that includes everything about you since you were little, pictures of you and your family and major events in your life is of interest only to people who know you personally. It is doubtful whether anyone else will visit the site, and even if they do, the information in it would have to be totally amazing or really funny if they are to spend more than two seconds in this kind of site.

It is better to make your personal site about a favorite hobby or some special talent you have, that other people will find interesting. It is worth thinking about who you would like your "target public" (the people who will visit your site) to be and design the content to suit them.

It is very advisable that the subject of the Web site is something you are really interested in and that you understand, a subject that you can say something about. That is, a subject that you can write a text about and that you can back up with interesting material (images, audio or video clips).

Don't be tempted to build a site about something you are not really familiar with – you don't want to put your ignorance on show for the whole world. A subject that doesn't really interest you will make you abandon the site once you have finished it and gotten past the challenge of actually building it.

Since the main problem facing Web site builders (like you) is the content (which we will refer to later), I recommend that you choose a subject that you already have some material on.

As a school pupil you must surely have done several projects already on some topics. Now is the time to shake the dust off those school files and choose one of those projects that you can present digitally – on the Internet by building and publishing a Web site.

Collecting and preparing material

As soon as you have selected the subject for your Web site, it is time to collect the materials for it. The materials that are used to make Web sites are primarily text and images, combined with various files (software, audio or video files, etc.). Collecting materials for a Web site is a lot like collecting materials for a school project. But because you are using electronic means to present this project, you will be able to use materials that you would not be able to use if you were only typing up a print copy.

If you decide to make your site about a subject that you already did a project on in school, you probably used the word processor (for example: Microsoft Word). If you did, this makes building your site much easier, because you can copy material from your school files and paste it into Notepad.

If you have chosen to build a site about a particular subject, surf other sites on that subject. You can use search engines for this by typing in key words for a search on that topic. Check out the content of the sites that come up and see what is good in them, what is bad and what is missing.

Plan your own site to include valueable information from those sites and collect more material to cover what is missing. But don't copy material from any other site without permission. You can translate material from sites in other languages, but first you must read what is written in the Restrictions on Usage (Terms of Use page) in that Web site.

You will need **graphics**, which you can either prepare yourself or download from the Internet. Your own PC contains some software (Paintbrush) that will enable you to create simple and attractive graphics. But for more impressive and professional results you will need graphics software like Photoshop or Paint Shop Pro (they are the most popular in the field). There are also sites that offer collections of graphics free of charge.

To find images (buttons, bars, icons, pictures…) that are free of charge and that you can make free use of, go to one of the search engines and type in **free graphics** or **free images**. If you find a picture you like there:

1. Read what is written in the Restrictions on Usage (Terms of Use page) in the Web site that you want to copy from.

2. Position the cursor on the picture, right click with the mouse and select **Save Picture As….** Save the picture in the picture folder of your Web site.

You can collect material at random or with a definite plan in mind, but eventually you will have to make a map of your Web site or a content list, and divide up the materials between the different pages of the site. Just as you would like to get an A grade for your school project, you should aim for the highest standard in your Web site too. But one of the differences between this and a school project is that on your Web site, if something is missing or you are not satisfied with the results, you can always add to it and improve it even after the site is completed.

Even if you have the greatest content and the most wonderful files to go with it, you will want to present it well. Make sure that there are neither content errors nor spelling mistakes in the texts you include in your site, and that the grammar is correct too. It is a good idea to run a computer Spell Check on the texts, but you should also print out all the pages and proofread them yourself. It is easier and more convenient to read them on paper than on the screen. You have a better chance of finding mistakes this way.

Design your Web site

The first thing that surfers will notice on your Web site is the design (the "look and feel"). Before they read even one word, they see the **site design** and that is why this subject is no less important than content. A site must offer surfers not only interesting content, as explained above, but must also provide a pleasant visual experience.

The site's appearance should be appropriate to its content. There should be some connection between the content and the way it looks. For instance, the design of a site commemorating the events of September 11th will be conservative, its graphics will be moderate, it will not have small pop-up windows that distract attention and it won't contain advertisements. Otherwise the surfer will feel that the message transmitted by the text and the message transmitted by the visual design are incompatible.

On the other hand, on the Web site of a clown who performs for birthdays, everything that is unsuitable for use on a memorial site may be used – and more. On a clown's site, everything should be colorful, happy, surprising and it should be accompanied by music and animation.

There is no such thing as "no design." Even a site consisting of black letters on a white background has a design.

The design of the Web site should suit its content, including files that accompany it (images, video and audio clips, etc.). Images should match the text. Do not use pictures where the surfer will have difficulty understanding the subject of the photograph.

Now that you have the materials (text and images), you need to plan your Web site. The structure of your first site should be simple. When you were little you used to do puzzles with only four pieces. Now that you are a teenager you can do puzzles with 500 pieces, or even more. It is the same with building a Web site on the Internet. Start with a simple structure.

Justin's personal Web site, which you built in the course of this book, is structured as follows:

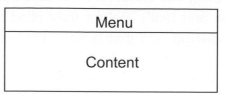

So logically, it looks like this:

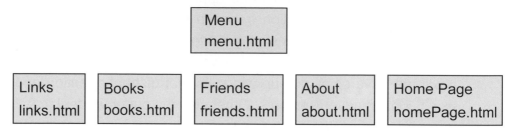

This is a "flat" structure with links from the menu to each of the pages.

At least at the initial stage, keep to a similar flat structure for your own site too. Your site may contain more than the number of files indicated. Regardless of the number of pages, the main idea is to keep it simple.

Building your own Web site on your PC

Now that you have all the materials (text and images) and you have designed your Web site, it's time to build. You can use the pages you already built in Justin's Web site to help you. Just copy some of the files – or all of them if you prefer – from the **justin** folder to the new folder that you just opened.

Let's say that you want to build a site about a baseball team. One of the pages will be about the players. For every pitcher, catcher, infielder and outfielder you want to show an image and some text. For that purpose you can use the books.html or friends.html Web pages from Justin's Web site. Replace the images, change the text and…you have a Web page!

Use the book as a reference manual while building your Web site. Go back to the stages you need to be reminded of, whether they are choosing a color, creating a table, adding an image, formatting a text, etc. Now, that you are familiar with the book and with Justin's Web site you can say: "I want to do that", then locate the appropriate page(s) in the book and see how to do it.

Applying minimal loading time

Try to keep your site "compact" – this means using small images and small image size. Images that load onto your computer quickly will take much longer when your Web site will be on the Internet. A 500Kb picture that loaded onto your PC in what seemed like the blink of an eye will be much slower on the Internet. The slow loading time will irritate surfers and they will not wait for the images to load. Instead, they will move on to another site. That is why you should keep your images small. A 10Kb image size is reasonable. You can have more than one image on any page, but bear in mind that you should not surpass 70Kb total image size per page. You can add some larger images and let surfers know that they will have to wait until they finish loading.

Upload your site onto the Internet

Part II deals with this subject.

Maintenance

The Internet is a great big cemetery for Web sites that were discarded by people who built them. I hope this is not the fate that you wish for your own Web site. When you walk around a shopping mall, you notice that window displays in the stores are changed regularly. This should be the case with your site too. Every so often (you will decide how often: daily, weekly or by-annually), you should do something to vary your site if you want people to come back for a return visit.

You must show returning surfers something new. The least you can do is change the design: color, position of headings, etc. You can also add and/or update content and offer new services.

Summary

The only way of the measuring success of an Internet site is through repeat traffic by loyal users. In order to do this you have to remember that these are the four things that users want more than anything else:

◎ Quality content

◎ Ongoing updates

◎ Minimal loading time

◎ Easy, convenient use

Now – go ahead and use the information you learned during the process of building Justin's Web site and build your own Web site.

Good luck!

Part II
Web site Hosting

Part II

Web Site Hosting

Making your site LIVE!

At this stage you already have a Web site ready on your PC at home – Justin's personal site and/or your own Web site.

Is your Web site ready? Do you want to upload it onto the Internet? That is the obvious thing to do now, otherwise no one else will be able to see it except for those using your home PC. In order for the HTML pages that you prepared to become a "Web site," they must be accessible to surfers throughout the Web. This is done by giving your Web site an address which usually begins with the letters **www**. Anything else is not a Web site.

You need to store your Web site files (HTML and images files) on a computer on the World Wide Web that is called a **server** – as opposed to your computer which requests and receives data and is called a **client**. The server must be secure, that is, it should have a degree of **data security**. You don't want other people to be able to access your Web site and make changes to it, do you?

The server you choose to store your files on must be operative 24/7: 24 hours a day, 7 days a week, 365 days a year.

And what about response times? Anyone typing your address expects the Web site to open in less than 10 seconds. If it doesn't, they will probably lose their patience and move on to another site. Response times must be reasonable, so you need to be sure that the server has the necessary **infrastructure** for this.

Some storage sites restrict access to your site. They may have restrictions on traffic, the transmission from a server to a client; or they might restrict the number of entries, such as 10 entries per day.

There are also storage sites that are copyrighted and do not permit storage and downloading of certain types of files.

How to find a free storage site

1. Go to your favorite search engine.

2. In the Search window type the words (all or part of them): **free Web hosting services**.

3. Click on **Go** or **Search** or whatever is written on the button that launches the search.

See chapter 13 for more details on how to find free hosting.

How to upload a Web site onto the Internet

The list below explains the stages of this process. It applies to most Web sites.

1. Register with a server that supplies storage service.

2. Receive or choose a user name and password.

3. By return e-mail you will receive confirmation of your registration and the address to which you can upload your files onto a Web site (via ftp or browser).

4. Access the Web site at the address that was allocated and by the means that were selected (either ftp or browser).

5. Upload the files to the site.

See chapter 13 for more details on how to upload your Web site.

I have more questions

You may have more questions such as:

◎ My name is Nicholas and I would like the address of my Web site to be **www.nicholas.com**. How do I do that?

◎ On the server where I am storing my Web site, is it possible to have mail boxes? Is there a hit counter?

◎ What is the best method for uploading files to the server?

◎ How can I measure the response time of the storage site?

◎ Does "free" really mean free?

Chapter 13 provides you the answers to these questions.

Selecting a Web Hosting Server

Congratulations! If you have reached this chapter of the book, you probably already have a Web site prepared on your home PC. The Internet enables you to publicize your content and express your creativity at a laughable price, if any. Additionally, you display the contents of your Web site to a public that is potentially many times larger than any other advertising medium you have ever known.

Is your Web site ready? Do you want to put it on the Internet? That is obviously the next step; otherwise no one else would be able to see it, except those who use your PC. In order for the HTML pages that you prepared to become a "Web site", they must be accessible to everyone on the Internet. This is achieved by giving your "Web site" an address. If this is not done, it is not a Web site.

The Internet is a giant, unlimited stage that is prepared to accept any Web site and any content. It is a network of computer networks that provides access to every individual in the world, from any computer, from any place on earth, provided that he or she is connected to the Internet.

Communication between computers enables the transfer of information between users, this is usually done by means of e-mail or forums, and accessing information stored on other computers connected to the Internet. Communication between computers on the Internet consists of servers & clients. The computer providing the information is called a server and the computer requesting and receiving the information is called a client.

For example: Internet surfers are clients because their computers request information from a server computer on the internet and the server computer on the Internet responds to these requests.

The HTTP protocol, through which contact is made on the Internet, is a request / response protocol. Even when the user is transfering information (by e-mail or instant messaging), the user is still a client because there is no sharing of information stored on the individual computer.

Even your PC can become a server, providing access for other surfers to the information it contains (different types of files such as HTML documents, Word documents, PowerPoint presentations, pictures, etc.) However, you should take into account several factors including the following:

◎ **Information security** – Are you prepared to open the "door" to your personal computer to everyone? Are you prepared to risk the privacy and integrity of the information in your personal computer? Are you prepared for the possibility of damage to your information? When was the last time you backed up your data?

◎ **Availability** – Your computer is supposed to provide service 24 hours a day. This involves two main things: One, your PC must be connected to the Internet 24 hours a day, 365 days a year. Two, you must be sure that it is operating 24 hours a day. You know from personal experience that computers, including yours, crash, get stuck or just don't respond from time to time.

◎ **Infrastructures** – Up to this point, building your site has been free or relatively inexpensive. Turning your PC into a server on the Internet obligates you to purchase a few products including: Internet server (software), an IP address and a domain name. This configuration will enable users to roam around your computer (we've already mentioned security). For this reason you will need an operating system like Windows NT/200x with some kind of protection, as well as a router (hardware), a firewall (hardware & software) and a permanent fast connection.

There are other considerations as well (response time, number of simultaneous users, etc.) but the main considerations noted above may lead you to the conclusion that turning your home PC into an Internet server is not a good idea. It is better to find a free Web hosting server on the Internet for your Web site.

This chapter will help you select the best Web hosting server for your Web site taking into consideration the conditions you require and the conditions which are available to you, with the emphasis on finding a Web hosting server for **FREE**.

Some things you should know before selecting a host for your Web site

This information targets private users who are interested in putting a private Web site on the Internet. The information is NOT suitable for someone who is interested in putting an e-commerce Web site since subjects like safety, information security, shopping cart and billing are NOT in the scope of this chapter.

This chapter does not claim to provide you with all the possibilities for putting a Web site on the Internet. There are, of course additional possibilities that are not mentioned here, but this is the nature of the Internet, which is constantly developing and changing and offering new services. This chapter will give you guidelines to examine those services.

The Internet is always "alive and kicking": new Web sites appear, old Web sites disappear (they're removed) and others are simply deserted. New services are offered, others are upgraded and more than one has simply been abandoned. Most services on the Internet are provided free of charge, but some are provided for a fee. What is provided free today may not necessarily be free tomorrow.

The Internet is virtual, but behind it stand real people and commercial companies and there too, things are happening. New companies offer their services, others merge, downsize or close their Web sites. You should therefore view this chapter of the book as a basis from which to investigate the Internet – all the information is actually there.

If all the information is on the internet, why do you need to continue reading?

Reading this chapter is like setting out on a treasure hunt with a map and clues. This chapter will prepare you for the possibilities that you may encounter. It will present you with the alternatives so that you will not get stuck suddenly, for example, when you realize that there is a problem with the type of files that you want to upload to the Web hosting server or access or obtaining services or response times. There can be many problems during the registration process, when uploading the material and even afterwards, during use.

While it is true that many Web hosting servers provide support to the potential client, the support is specific to the Web hosting site from which you are requesting information and even then only after you register. Most of the Web hosting servers that charge a fee, provide support as part of the service given to the client, but that does not always mean round-the-clock support... There are many more problems you may encounter, and it is simply worth knowing about them before you decide that you want to use their Web hosting services.

How do you search for free Web Hosting Services?

1. Go into your favorite search engine.

2. In the search box, type the words (all or part of them):

   free Web hosting services

3. Click the **Search/Go** button.

How to register to Web hosing service?

Below are the stages of the process. They apply to most Web hosting services:

1. Register with a Web hosting server that provides Web hosting (either for a fee or free of charge).

2. Receive or choose a User Name (code) and Password.

3. Receive by return e-mail, registration confirmation and the address to which you can upload your files to a Web host folder (by FTP or by browser).

4. Log on to the site at the address you received and by the means you selected (FTP or browser).

5. Upload the files to the Web host folder.

What is a Web hosting server and why is it necessary?

No matter how good the Web site is, it is worthless unless it is placed on the Internet. In other words if the Web site you built is located on your PC and does not have an accessible IP address it will not be available to anyone but you. To enable access for other people to your Web site it must be hosted on a computer that is operational 24 hours a day and is part of the Internet.

Internet Service Providers (ISPs), for example, enable you to build and store your personal Web site on their computers. A Web hosting server is actually a computer with a Windows NT/200x or Unix/Linux operating system and Internet Server software. This computer has permanent high speed access to the Internet (a much broader bandwidth than what you get at home).

The Web sites stored on the Web hosting server are located on the server's hard disk. Each site is located in a separate folder. The Web sites operate within and from the server – just the same way your Web site works from your computer. In reality, thousands of Web sites can be hosted on one Web hosting server. So the problem that

Web hosting servers must contend with is not storage space, but rather user traffic to and from the Web sites. That is the factor that aggravates the server and slows down its operation.

ISPs are usually companies that offer, in addition to Web hosting, Web site building services or communications packages. There are many companies that sell Web hosting services, with a wide variety of programs and prices, and there are also companies that provide Web hosting services free of charge.

So right from the start you are faced with the question: If there are FREE Web hosting services, why pay for the service? A "better" question is: Why do companies provide free Web hosting? What do they get out of it? Where is the "catch"? Does "free of charge" really mean… free? After all, everyone knows that "you get what you pay for!" What does this "freebie" include?

There are companies (Web hosting services) whose business is based on regular large-scale clients that pay for services. This enables them to offer their "surplus" free of charge (disk space, Web traffic).

Sometimes, an offer to provide Web hosting services free of charge is an attempt to "trap" the client. Behind the free offer can be strategies such as: "Now it's free of charge, tomorrow you'll have to pay" (for example, a newspaper Web site that plans to collect payment for some parts of the site), or policies such as: "Now you will receive something for free; when you want additional services or an upgrade of the existing ones – we'll send you a price quotation" (for example Hotmail. Hotmail is a FREE e-mail service, but you have to pay if you want to enlarge your e-mail box).

If you, the Web site owner, do not pay, who does? The answer is: the advertiser. Companies that offer free Web hosting services sell advertising space. You are familiar with advertising on the Internet from passive ads that include banners across the screen – at the top, on the side, in every possible position – to active ads that flash, pester, irritate, and pop up with no advance warning and take up most of the screen. Sometimes the only way to escape them is to disconnect from the Internet and/or switch off your computer. These types of advertisements are called pop-ups. You have a free Web site, but your users will have to strain their eyes to find the content of your Web site among all the banners and pop-ups, and the chance of those users remaining or returning is small.

There are Web hosting services that offer a free deal (for now…), without third party advertising (in the meantime…). Their condition for this free deal is that their advertising will appear on your Web site.

If someone offers you Web hosting services free of charge – you must try to understand what is behind the offer and whether you are prepared to accept the conditions.

If they don't suit you, you can search for a better free offer or look for a Web hosting service that charges a fee.

What is a domain name?

A domain name is the address of an Internet Web site. For example, www.nba.com is a domain name and www.bookchamp. net is a domain name too. www.jaguarusa.com/us/en/home.htm is the address of a page named home.htm in a domain name called www.jaguarusa.com in a folder named "us" in a sub-folder named "en".

In effect, the address of an Internet Web site is an IP address. An IP address is a series of 4 numbers. Each number goes from 0 to 255. These 4 numbers are seperated by dots. For example, 64.241.25.66 is the IP address of the National Park Service Web site. If you type 64.241.25.66 in the address bar of the browser and press Enter, it will be exactly like typing www.nps.com. So which is easier for you to remember: 64.241.25.66 or www.nps.com? We are people, not machines, so it's easier for us to both remember and type www.nps.com. But the TCP/IP protocol recognizes only numbers (0…9), and the job of a domain system is to translate an address consisting of words (www.nps.com) into an IP address in figures (64.241.25.66).

When you type an Internet address in the browser address bar (for example, www.ci.sf.ca.us) and then press Enter, your request is transferred to the Internet and at a certain stage in the process it must be translated into an IP address (in figures) because it is only by means of an IP address that computers can communicate on the Internet. If you have a domain name, it must be connected to an IP address. The IP address is a unique address on the Internet. You can connect more than one domain name to a single IP address. For example, www.iloveny.com and www.state.co.us are two different domain names that are connected to the same IP address (205.232.252.58).

Selecting a domain name

One of the main problems in selecting a domain name (and naturally, also in buying one) is that most of the "good" names are already registered and are therefore unavailable. A good domain name is one with some special meaning or one that is related to the Web site content. For example, the domain name of the Web site for Ford is www.ford.com; and the Web site of the Disney Company is www.disney.com. It is best to have a domain name that is not too long. A long name is problematic because most Internet surfers will not remember it or will spell and/or type it incorrectly. A good name is worth money. A short, catchy name enables users to type the Web site name by themselves and not to use a link from a search engine or another source.

◎ A short name – Learn from the experience of the bookstore www.barnesandnoble.com. It is much easier to write the name as follows: www.bn.com.

◎ A meaningful name – not obligatory, but desirable. If your Web site is about food, it's best for it to have a name like, food, efood,

food4you, netfood and so forth, naturally with the prefix "www" and the extension ".com"

Another important item is how to check whether the domain name is already registered (unavailable). It's not enough to type in the domain name and see if the site opens. Sometimes, someone has already bought the domain name but is not using it for various reasons. There are Web sites that sell and trade in domain names. Usually these Web sites have a special search engine that checks whether the domain name is free for use. If the domain name is unavailable, you may be offered an alternative with a different ending, for example, "net" instead of "com" or you may be offered other, similar options that are available. For example, since the domain name "baseball.com" is unavailable, you will be offered "baseball. vg" or "dumpbaseball.com". Just by adding a letter or a number, the domain name is yours.

There are Web sites that can locate the domain owner and will even offer to negotiate between you and the domain name owner to enable you to buy that domain name.

It is not only the domain name that attests to the content of the Web site but also the extension (".com") of the domain name. It's best to buy a domain name that ends with ".com" if the Web site is in English and is aimed for US users. If ".com" cannot be obtained, the next possibility is ".net". The reason for this is that people only remember the name of the Web site and not its extension, and they will write the common extension ".com".

The following extensions can be used in accordance with the content of your site:

.com – commercial   **.net** – Internet Service Provider

.org – non-profit group   **.biz** – business

.us – American Web site   **.gov** – governmental

.info – credible resource

Don't be tempted to buy a domain name that ends with "us" or "biz" which are usually available, unless the Web site requires it.

Sub-domain

There are Web hosting services that allow you to select your User Name. This name becomes a central component in your Web site sub-domain:

www.somedomain.com/members/yourname

This sub-domain is the address of your Web site. Instead of "yourname" there can be a number or text or a combination of the two.

Since the sub-domain is long anyway, because it includes the name of the company that is providing the Web hosting services, it is best to select a short, catchy User Name, or to shorten the address.

ReDirect to the address

Just like a shortcut on the Desktop in a Windows operating system, you can make a shortcut to your own Web site. This shortcut is called "shortURL" or "ReDirect". Let's assume that your Web site is located, physically, at the address (the part in bold is the fixed part that cannot be changed):

www.domainOne.com/members/games/yourName

You can buy (or get free of charge) a ReDirect called: **name.domainTwo.com**

Someone surfing the Internet who wants to find your Web site will type name.domainTwo.com, but will be referred to www.domainOne.com/members/games/yourName.

This free service provides a simple and easy-to-remember Web address that transfers (redirects) users to the location of your Web site.

The considerations in selecting a ReDirect for the Web site are the same considerations in selecting a domain name. Here too, most of the good abbreviations (short names) are already registered and are therefore not available, although due to the wide variety of Web hosting companies offering ReDirects, you may be able to find the best abbreviated name in another Web hosting company.

See the list of Web sites in Appendix A.

Buying a domain name

Buying a domain name costs money. There are many Web hosting services that sell domain names in the US and abroad. The purchase is usually for the first two years, and after that the price goes down. Ownership of the domain name must be renewed every two years.

How much does a domain name cost?

The price of a regular address is usually something around $20 for every two years (prices are controlled and vary from time to time). Addresses with a special extension, like. TV, cost more.

Where do I buy a domain name?

It is best to buy a domain from a reliable company. Look at **www.internic.com**.

How to purchase?

This is a straightforward process and you need a credit card in order to make the purchase. You will also need to provide your personal information (name, address, telephone number) and e-mail address. As with any purchase made via the Internet, check the following:

◎ The identity of the owner of the Web hosting service from which you are making the purchase (name, address, telephone number) is displayed openly.

- ◎ That the Web hosting service owner openly declares their privacy policy and tells you how they will handle information you provide.

- ◎ That the transfer of data is secure (a closed lock appears in the status bar, the address begins with https instead of http from the very outset of the process).

Finding a suitable Web hosting server

What are your options?

Use your existing Internet Service Provider. If your ISP, your school or the place where your parents work already maintains a Web server, check to see whether you can put your Web site there and check to see how you can copy your documents (files) to that server. That kind of Web hosting service is usually free of charge.

Rent space on a Web hosting server. This service can be given free of charge or for payment, from a relatively small fee per month up to several thousand US dollars.

It is NOT recommended to turn your own computer into a server, something we already discussed and advised against at the beginning of this chapter.

What types of Web hosting services exist?

You can obtain Web hosting services for a fee or free of charge. Each of these options comes with features that you should know about so that you will be able to match your requirements to the features of the Web hosting site. Whether you choose a Web hosting server for a fee or free of charge, you should check the following things:

1. **What is the storage space (disk space, disk storage) they offer?** Most of the Web hosting servers (free of charge or for a fee) offer Web hosting packages generally starting from 5MB to 200MB and even more. The storage space must be compatible with the size of the Web site folder in your PC, and it is usually

best to plan for more storage space. If your Web site is expected to grow, look for a server that gives you the option of increasing your basic package to another convenient package, or take a package with more storage space to begin with.

2. **What type of Web hosting server is offered?** There are two main types of Web hosting servers – servers whose operating system is Windows NT/200x and those using UNIX/Linux. Most of the free Web hosting servers usually do not specify to clients the type of operating system their server uses and it really isn't important to you if you are interested in putting a site on the Internet that is entirely HTML. If you need server services (like SQL, ASP), then it is important to know the type of operating system so that you will be able to check that there is, indeed, support for any services you need.

   The difference between Windows NT/200x and UNIX/Linux servers is that Windows NT/200x servers are less "sensitive" and there is no need to be careful about case-sensitive text. With Windows NT/200x servers, it is not important what type of letters you use to write the name of the Web page (uppercase or lowercase). But this is not the case with UNIX/Linux servers. Since your site is (most likely) built on a Windows system, it is almost certain that it will work on a Windows NT/200x server. It can also work on a UNIX/Linux server if you make all the letter cases in the file names uniform. As a rule, Web hosting services on Windows NT/200x servers cost more.

3. **What languages does the server support?** Interactive Web sites based on a database (such as SQL or mySQL) use additional languages. The languages common today are PHP, Perl, CGI and ASP. However, most of the free servers do not support them and/or do not enable their use.

4. **Does the Web hosting service enable the use of a domain or a sub-domain?** Most of the free Webs hosting services offer a sub-domain as part of their sales promotion. There are even

paid Web hosting services that collect an additional amount for the use of a personal domain name. There are very few free Web hosting servers that will be prepared to let you use your private domain name. The problem is that the Web site address of the sub-domain becomes long and complicated and that makes it difficult to remember. One possible solution is the use of a short URL, or a ReDirect. This is a free service than enables you, the Web site owner, to select a shorter, catchier address for your Web site than the one offered by the free server.

5. **Is there e-mail service?** Most of the Web hosting servers that charge a fee, offer e-mail as part of the service to clients who are hosted by them, with an address for the domain.

The number of e-mail accounts that the client receives depends on the quality and size of the package purchased. It is best to take a package that includes one or more e-mail accounts. In other words, if Internet surfers want to e-mail the Web site, they can write to an address whose extension is the name of the Web site. Most of the free Web hosting servers do not provide e-mail as an integral part of the Web site. There are sites that offer their members a range of free services (they are usually large portals or Internet Service Providers), including e-mail and storage space, however these are not interdependent. In other words, there does not have to be a connection (in spelling) between your e-mail and the domain/sub-domain name.

6. **Does the Web hosting server provide you with statistics (traffic stats, Web site reports)?** Most of the free Web hosting services do not provide statistics such as the number of hits, where the visitors came from, which pages are most frequently visited, the length of time each visitor spends on the site, etc. Some Web hosting services provide a hit counter that counts the number of visitors, not visits, to the site (even if you visit a site 20 times in the same month, you will be counted only once), and there are those that count the number of clicks on the site – in other words, the number of requests for pages. If people

make your Web site their home page on their browsers, then every time they open the browser, the counter on your Web site will grow by 1 (one) and if they open the same home page 20 times in one day, your counter will grow by 20. This process is called clicks.

Statistics can include information on the type of browsers used by visitors to your Web site, the resolution of their screen, the Web site from which they reached your Web site, their IP address, how many pages they viewed on your Web site, etc. With some of the fee-charging Web hosting services this is included in the package, with others you must pay an additional charge for this service, and some do not provide such a service at all.

Most of the free Web hosting servers do not provide either counters or statistics services.

7. **Does the server give you technical support?** There are Web hosts that provide no support at all, others provide support at certain hours on certain days, and others provide service round the clock. Notice that the technical support is by e-mail, phone or both. The best, of course, is a Web host that provides 24 hour support.

8. **Does the Web hosting server provide back-up and recovery services in case of breakdown or hacking?** Most of the free servers do not provide these services and even the servers who charge a fee, do not always include backup services in the package that they offer. You should make a note of the backup times and frequency (daily, weekly or monthly) because recovery will only be up to the last date on which the Web site was backed up and not necessarily the date on which it crashed.

9. **Does the Web hosting server enable unrestricted visitor traffic on the Web site?** Some Web hosting companies impose restrictions on the number of visitors accessing the Web site at any one time. This is particularly common among free servers in

an effort to avoid overloading their servers. There are sites that restrict the number of clicks on the Web site. When a particular Web site exceeds that number of clicks or some other number, the host closes and a visitor arriving at your Web site will receive a message such as: "Web site is currently unavailable. Try again later".

10. **Does the Web hosting server restrict the size of data transferred by the Web site (data transfer)?** There is another type of traffic restriction (monthly bandwidth, Web traffic) which is more common on Web sites that charge a fee, and that is the amount of usage of the server.

Every request of information from the server is actualy copying and not moving files from the web server to the visitor's computer. These files are usually HTML files and images, but may also consist of files downloaded from the Web site, such as MP3 files, presentations or any other file transferred between the server and the client. These files are also counted towards server usage. Downloading files creates a load on the server, which requires additional payment for the increased use. On the free servers that restrict traffic of this type, it is best not to enable visitors to download files, and also to minimize the size of the pictures.

11. **What are the means of uploading a Web site to the Internet?** There are two possibilities for uploading material onto the Web site:

◎   File Transfer Protocol (FTP client or Web-base FTP) or

◎   Browser form.

The way to upload material to the server depends on the options offered by the Web hosting server. The fastest way is by FTP upload. FTP enables you to upload entire folders of files to the server, which makes the uploading process simple and fast. Generally, when uploading files by means of the browser (form), only one file can be uploaded (an HTML file, picture and so forth) at a time. There are sites that enable the uploading of a larger number of files, but generally no more than five files simultaneously, which prolongs the process of copying files to the server.

12. **What is the response time of the Web site?** The speed at which an HTML page is downloaded (when a client requests your Web page, he is downloading it from the Web hosting server), is a function of several variables: size of the file (HTML page, but mainly pictures), speed of the server on which the Web site is hosted, type of user's connection, etc. The server's speed is a function of the manner in which the server is connected to the Internet – the type of communication line that is connected to it, and how broad it is.

It also depends on the number of Web sites hosted on that server or, more accurately, the number of users who want to get to those Web sites. If we imagine the server's connection to the Internet as a highway, then Internet surfers who use that highway, who want to reach the sites on the server, are the cars. The more cars on the highway, the slower the traffic (lower speed).

The response time of the Web site depends on the size of the files transferred between visitors to the Web hosting server. Imagine that some of the visitors are traveling in trucks, not cars. That increases the load on the road and slows down the speed of the traffic. The speed of the Web hosting server can be checked by using a ping software, which checks the amount of time it takes for the Web hosting server to respond. The program gives the server's response time in thousandths of a second. If you use a ping software to decide which Web hosting company to choose, remember that the speed of the server is not fixed and depends on the load on the Internet. It is also not recommended to check the home page of the Web hosting company, but rather the Web sites that the company is hosting, since most of the companies give better conditions to themselves than to the Web sites that they host. Another way to check, is to visit Web sites hosted on that server at various times and to take note of the speed – it's not scientific, it's not precise, but it's good enough.

13. **A server locally based or a server in another state?** An important point to remember is that the geographical location of the server changes the speed of the response and transfer of the information to the visitor.; The use of a server that is located closer is an advantage.

14. **What other tools does the Web hosting server offer?** There are Web hosting servers that provide additional tools for building the Web site and maintaining it on the Internet.

    For example, they provide a wizard (site builder tool) for building HTML pages, tools to check the Web site (for example, programs that check that all the links that you've written lead somewhere), means for promoting the Web site (distributing the Web site on the search engines).

Servers that charge a fee, or What you won't get with a free server

Read this section even if you do not intend to pay. But don't take our word for it – check it.

Why is it worth choosing a Web hosting server that charges a fee?

The prestige of the Web site increases when it has its own domain, when it is conveniently accessible to all visitors and when it does not carry advertisements of the Web hosting server. When a Web site has databases managed by the server, its complexity increases and it requires more services. Web site owners who consider themselves builders of professional Web sites prefer to host a Web site on Web hosting servers that have no traffic restrictions, no advertisements, and that support a variety of languages and tools. No server gives all these advantages for free.

Safety and security

Usually, a Web site that is hosted on a paid Web hosting server is more secure than a Web site hosted on a free server. You should check whether the payment includes backup, recovery and firewall services.

For Web site that use a database, backup and recovery is vital. With a static Web site built of HTML pages, that is located on your PC, you can do a backup yourself.

The server owner will inform his paid customers of any problem (for example, traffic volume problems) and will give them the opportunity to make changes. This is not the case with free sites. If a condition in the contract is breached, your Web site may be closed, even without any advance warning.

If the server crashes, a Web sites with pay will be handled immediately and will be redirected to operate from the backup server, while Web sites hosted on a server that provides free service will have to wait until the server is back online.

Technical support

Will you need support in uploading the Web site and maintaining it on the server? Most of the Web hosts that charge a fee provide support for their clients (the Web site owners), some of them 24 hours a day. That is not true for those who choose free Web hosting, where there is sometimes no support at all, and when there is support, no one will knock themselves out to help you. That means that you will get an answer, but sometimes only three business days later.

Files

Another advantage in using Web hosting servers that charge a fee is that they allow to store large-volume files. Most of the Web hosting services are prepared and even want to host programs and files, since the price of most Web hosting package are determined by the size of the space that is rented, and files (videos, mp3) take up much more disk space than HTML pages. Most of the free servers restrict the type, quantity and size of the files that they will host. Very few free sites are prepared to host EXE and MP3 type files, primarily due to the fear of violating copyrights.

Connectivity and reliability

There is no point in putting your Web site on a Web hosting server that cannot be accessed or that has slow access. A Web hosting server that crashes every other day annoys not only you, the Web site owner, but also the visitors who are trying to access your Web site and are receiving a message that the Internet page is not available. A server that is too slow may also discourage visitors, who will lose patience while waiting for your Web site to load. The Web hosting companies give priority to Web site owners who pay a fee; they are also placed on the faster server so their Web sites are more available. This is not the case with Web sites that are hosted for free.

What is the price and how is the calculation made?

The price of Web site hosting depends on all the factors mentioned previously. In principle, the minimum price to host a Web site is a few dollars a month. The price increases according to the number of services included in the package (storage space, Web traffic, backup, database support, statistics, etc).

In general, there are two main factors for calculating the price of the Web hosting package: a fixed price for storage space (disk space); and a price based on Web traffic (monthly bandwidth) from your Web site. Many Web hosting servers charge a fixed price for the storage space and an additional variable price depending on the traffic. The more traffic from your Web site, the more you pay. Therefore, selecting the Web hosting company and the type of package depends on the type of Web site that you want to put on the Internet. For example, a Web site that is composed mainly of text and few graphics does not require much storage space, but if its content is attractive, it can draw a lot of traffic, with payment calculated accordingly. In such a case, it is best to search for a Web hosting company that offers a fixed-price Web hosting package according to storage space, and not according to Web traffic.

Generally, the payment for hosting the Web site is made per month, but payment for three months or a year in advance may lower the monthly price.

Before you choose a server that charges a fee, there are things you need to check:

1. **How reliable is the server you are considering?** After all, you don't want to risk your Web site and your money. With that in mind, how do you check the reliability of the Web hosting server? First, check to see who the other clients are. A Web hosting server that hosts large, well-known Web sites is probably reliable. It is also worth speaking to the Webmaster of one of the clients who will tell you everything you wanted to know but were afraid to ask.

2. **Is there 24 hour support?** As long as you're paying, why not get the best – round-the-clock support. If there is no round-the-clock support, check to see if the support hours are compatible with the hours you are online.

3. **Will you be able to use your domain or sub-domain?** As long as you're paying and you have your own domain, it's best to go with a Web hosting company that will connect an IP address to the domain name that you purchased. If you don't have a domain name, every Web hosting company will be happy to give you a sub-domain.

4. **Do you need a server-side scripting languages?** If you need ASP support, you will need to look for a server whose operating system is Windows NT/200x. Windows NT/200x servers are more expensive, so if you are comparing Web hosting packages, compare those with identical operating systems that support the

same languages. If you need CGI, Perl or PHP look for a Unix/Linux Web host server.

5. **Do you have many files or just a few?** Check whether you will have to pay more for storing accompanying files and whether the Web hosting server calculates the storage of different types of files in different ways.

6. **How do you upload files? By FTP or through the browser?** Copying files by FTP is preferable because it is faster and more reliable. This method uses the protocol that is designed for copying files (FTP) and not the protocol that is designed for transferring images and text (HTTP).

7. **Do you want a fast server or would you be satisfied with a medium speed server?** It is highly probable that the faster the server, the more expensive the package will be, since speed is also a part of the price.

8. **What is the server's response time?** As explained earlier, you can check this by means of a ping command. There are Web sites that offer to check the response speed of Web sites for you. The values obtained from a ping command are in thousandths of a second.

   If you get a result lower than 150, it means that it's a very fast server. A result lower than 400 means it's a fast server. A server that responds in a range from 400 to 700 is defined as a medium speed server. A server whose response speed is over 700 thousandths of a second, it is considered a slow server and is not recommended. It's worth sampling the site several times over the course of a day. You will be surprised at how the data can vary from one reading to another. You should be aware of the fact that there are Web sites that block ping service so that they will not be bothered. One of these, for example is www.microsoft.com.

9. **How many visitors to your Web site do you anticipate?** If you are expecting a large number of visitors to your Web site, choose a Web host server that does not charge extra for Web traffic.

10. **How much storage space do you currently need for your Web site and how much will you need in the future?** The size of the storage volume is not the only factor in calculating the payment for hosting the Web site. It's only part of it. The size of the storage space you require will always be the same size as, or larger than, the Web site folder on your PC. It is best to choose a Web hosting server whose basic package price is suitable and it is also desirable that the cost for added storage space is reasonable.

Free Web Hosting servers

Free on the Internet

The word "free" is a key word on the Internet and it's one of the most common search words. Not only do Internet surfers search for "free" stuff on the Internet, businesses also offer services for free. But is it really free?

You have to remember that the word "free" on the Internet means that users do not have to pay for services that they receive. However, in most cases you pay for these services in a different way. You must understand that someone has to "pay". The payment may not be made in money but it may be worth money. For example, you can receive a free e-mail account. When your mail is filled with weekly advertisements, you'll understand why they were so generous in giving you free e-mail. In about two weeks, you'll start receiving e-mail from companies you don't know and then you will understand that your e-mail address was sold to businesses, so it turns out that "free" is not exactly free. The Web hosting server which gave you a free e-mail account receives money from businesses that are prepared to pay to send e-mail directly to you. (Yes, I know what you're thinking! "I'll just open an e-mail account and they'll send all the advertisements there... ha, ha, ha." Did you think they haven't thought of that? You're not the first client who wants to "fix" them).

Advertisements are also common when your Web site is hosted for free, just like free e-mail. Visitors to the Web site are exposed to advertisements. Other services for Web site owners also entail exposing visitors to advertisements on the Web site. You can find every Web site building tool on the Internet for free, from building programs, graphics and other auxiliary tools, like a hit counter and statistics services, to forums, chat rooms, bulletin boards, guest books, surveys and more. Even "free" graphics, which are very common on the Internet, entail exposure to advertisements. Sometimes, you'll be asked to link the picture you received for free to the Web site from which you downloaded it, sometimes you will be asked to insert a small banner of the Web site. In the end, your Web site could look like a sponsorship Web site.

Before registering for any free service on the Internet, it is very important to read the fine print of the contract/agreement and see what conditions the company is offering you as a client and what it requires from you. Look for confidentiality. That means that they will not pass on your private information to another entity. Otherwise, your e-mail account may be flooded with junk mail.

Is it true that it doesn't cost any money?

Yes, free Web hosting does not require you, the Web site owner, to part with money in order to store your Web site on the server. A Web site can be hosted for free on the servers of institutions and organizations (a school, university, local authority, etc.), on the servers of commercial companies, on the servers of companies that provide Internet services (ISPs), on the servers of the portals, etc. So yes, there are freebies on the Internet.

What else does this "freebie" cost?

When we talk about a free Web hosting server, we usually mean the already constructed site of the server of a company that does not take payment from the client (that is you, the Web site owner).

But that does not mean that the Web hosting company loses by renting the space without payment. The space given free of charge exists on the server and when it is not active it does not bring in any income. However, if it is given, even without payment, a profit can still be made, for example from advertising. Thus, most of the free servers contain an advertising banner at the top of the page, at the bottom of the page or in a separate window that pops up each time the page is loaded. In effect, the Web site "pays" for its storage space. Money is not taken from you, the Web site owner, or from the visitors to the Web site, it is made from advertising.

There are Web hosting services that offer free service to Web sites only for certain subjects. For example, for small business Web sites, where the hosting service provides various business services to the Web site owners and earns fees as a broker.

Another reason why a particular company provides free Web hosting services is an attempt by such companies to trap the client. Certain sites provide a very small amount of space for free. This is the amount of space that is suitable for a newly launched Web site, but when the Web site grows and its owner needs more space, the user will be required to pay. The Web hosting company assumes that as soon as the Web site owner becomes accustomed to the services provided by the company, the user won't take the trouble to transfer to a different company and will prefer to pay and continue to maintain his Web site. Some of the companies rely on the laziness of the client (you, in this case), assuming that he will be prepared to pay rather than taking the trouble to search for a new Web hosting service. Restricting traffic is also a method of trapping the client.

You can also find free Web hosting space on the servers of various organizations and institutions. For example, many universities give their students free storage space for personal Web sites (this is the time to renew your relationship with your cousin who's in college, the one you haven't seen for years). There are also companies and enterprises that give their employees free Web hosting space (ask your parents or other relatives).

In most cases, the client's payment for the space is his undertaking to uphold certain conditions dictated by the server owner (restrictions on the Web site subject matter, the files it will contain and so forth).

Why and for whom is it worthwhile to use a free Web hosting server?

Why? Because it's free! However, it should be said that a free Web hosting service is not suitable for every Web site. There are Web sites whose contents require that they be on a server for a fee (for example, e-commerce Web sites). Web sites that want to show an aura of prestige and professionalism should not use free services because there is certain contempt for Web sites with advertising. The content of the advertisements may not be suitable for the content of the Web site. A Web site without a personal domain, which purports to be professional, does not appear reliable. In order to appear respectable and reliable, you have to invest!

Important! So who is the use of a free Web hosting server suitable for? Such use is suitable for small, private Web sites, for personal Web sites, for Web sites that are hobbies, for Web sites with little traffic, for nonprofit Web sites, for Web sites under construction or when the Web site owner wants to see how his Web site works on the Internet before he transfers it to a Web hosting server for a fee.

What are the services that you will receive for free?

The range of services that are found for free is not identical to those that can be obtained for payment. Most basic services can be obtained for free. Therefore, before choosing a Web hosting company, you must decide what is more important – a Web site without advertisements or a Web site without traffic restrictions, a Web site that supports server side languages or a Web site to which files can be uploaded by FTP, etc. Since these preferences are personal, the services should be examined carefully before you decide.

Before you choose a free Web hosting server, you should check the following things:

1. **Are there advertisements?** Most of the companies that provide free Web hosting services make money (or at least don't lose any) from the advertisements that they display on the Web site. Even though it's true that you can delete the advertising banners and prevent the advertising windows from opening, this can't be done on every Web site. Secondly, if they catch you doing this, your Web site will be deleted...

2. **Can you enter your Web site directly (by typing its address) or do you first go through the Web hosting server's home page?** Having to go through other home pages before getting to your own is not recommended at all.

3. **Do you have a lot of files?** This does not mean accompanying graphics files and not even sound files (midi or wav), but primarily MP3 and .EXE files. Storing large files, even of the mpeg and pps types, is problematic. Even if you succeed in uploading them to the Web site, it is not certain that your visitors will be able to download them afterwards. There are Web hosting servers in which you cannot store zip files, so look for restrictions regarding files on the Web site.

4. **Do you need a Web site that supports server side languages (CGI, ASP)?** Most of the free servers do not support these languages. While there are free servers that support languages, they restrict the Web hosting packages in another way (generally restricting Web traffic).

5. **How do you upload files to the Web hosting server?** Some of the free servers enable the use of FTP. On some you can

upload only by means of the browser (form). If the only option for uploading files is by means of the browser (form), it is best to know ahead of time how many files can be uploaded simultaneously.

6. **What is the server speed?** Naturally you want a fast server, but the question is whether, in a free deal, you can be satisfied with a medium speed server (of course, using a slow server is not recommended – even for free).

7. **How many visitors do you expect on your Web site?** It is not recommended to use Web hosting services that impose restrictions on Web site traffic because you can never know whether your Web site will be a hit or not. Also, a Web site with a large volume of visitor traffic is generally not suitable for a free server. Even regular Web hosting servers that don't restrict Web site traffic can threaten to close the Web site or demand payment when Web site traffic is very heavy, and the traffic volume overloads the server.

8. **Is there support?** The support given for a free Web site is not always inferior to the support given for Web sites that you pay for. Naturally, a server with support is preferable, but if there is no support – you can often get help in the chat rooms and forums of Internet Web site builders. Look for technical and how-to guides at the Web hosting site.

9. **How much storage space do you currently need for your Web site and how much will you need in the future?** There are Web hosting servers that provide Web hosting space in a large variety of sizes and there are even those that do not restrict the storage space (actually there is a restriction but it's not relevant to you).

Important note
Before registering for a Web hosting server, you must read the fine print of the contract/agreement and see what features the company offers

you and what it requires from you as a client. Never rely on the large print that appears on the opening page. Look inside in order to see what the conditions and features are.

Reading the fine print will tell you exactly what is permitted and what is prohibited on the Web site you are registering for. You can prevent unpleasantness, anger and frustration if you read it – do NOT forget the fine print (if necessary, use glasses, and if something in not 100% clear to you - ask your parents).

Uploading files to the Web hosting server

The files that make up your Web site, located on your PC, must be copied to the computer on which the Web site will be stored. There are two options for uploading files to the Web hosting server. The first option is to upload the files by :

◎   File Transfer Protocol (FTP client or Web-base FTP) or

◎   Browser form.

The fastest way is by FTP upload. You can Drag & Drop (copy) all the files from your Web site folder on your PC to the folder on the Web hosting server. If your Web site contains many files, it is more convenient to upload them to the Web hosting server by means of FTP.

Uploading files by FTP

What is FTP?

FTP is a service and also a software.

FTP software enables access to a Web hosting server via the Internet in a manner very similar to the use of Windows Explorer.

File Transfer Protocol (FTP) is a protocol (that is, a language for copying files between computers connected to the Internet), that enables the copying of files between various computers. This protocol works on the two-way server-client model in which the client can upload files to the server, download (copy) files from the server, delete files in the server, change the names of files located on the server, etc. Please note that in contrast to browser upload of files, you can also download from the server by means of an FTP interface.

When do you need to download files from the server? For example, when a particular file is corrupted on your PC and the only copy is on… the server.

The procedure for working with FTP software is:

1. The user connects to the Web hosting server (FTP server).

2. The use identifies himself with a User Name and Password.

3. The interface simulates two Windows Explorer windows: one shows the files in your local computer and the other shows the files in the Web hosting server. The work is very similar to working in Windows Explorer.

Recommended FTP software: WS_FTP or cuteFTP (these can be downloaded from www.tucows.com).

How do you upload files to the Web site by means of FTP software?

After registering with one of the Web hosting services, you will receive, by e-mail, a User Name, Password and address for your Web site. You will also receive the address of an FTP server that you must connect to.

When you open the FTP program there is a form on which you must fill in the details that you received. In the designated line, enter the address of the FTP server that you received from your Web hosting company, and afterwards User Name and Password.

Be sure that you have copied properly (It's best to use Ctrl+C and Ctrl+V in order to copy these details from your e-mail to the form). After filling in the necessary details make contact with the server by clicking Connect, this will connect you directly to your Web site folder on the server.

After making the connection, look on the left pane of the window (left side of the window) for the folder in which your Web site is stored. The left pane of the window displays your computer and the right pane of the window displays your folder on the Web hosting server which, at least in the beginning, should be empty.

Copy the files from the left pane to the right pane by means of the arrows or by Drag & Drop. In principle, work is now proceeding between these two panes and is the same as copying files between two folders in your computer. The original remains in the original folder and the copy is in another folder, only now the folder is on an Internet server.

In other FTP programs, you can highlight the desired files and drag them from window to window. You can send several files together by clicking more than one file simultaneously. You can also do other things with the files (for example, delete, view, change name, and so forth) by means of the buttons located on the right side of each of the windows.

Uploading files by means of the browser (form)

An alternative way of uploading files is using a browser inerface (form). You can select files and upload them to the Web hosting server. You can upload new files or update existing files by uploading a file of the same name and overwriting the existing file. Of course you can also delete a file. You can implement other functions such as transferring a file from one folder to another, and changing the name of a file and so forth if the hosting Web site allows you to do it by means of the interface.

The procedure for working with a browser is:

1. With your browser, enter the Web hosting site.

2. Identify yourself by User Name and Password.

3. A form-like interface is displayed and you can select one or more files (look for the Browse button).

4. Click the Submit button to copy the selected file(s) to the folder on a Web hosting server.

Use a form to upload a file throught the browser, but instead of filling in details such as name or e-mail, you type or select the name of the file that is located in your computer. The process of selecting the file is similar to the process of opening a document with your text editor or the process of selecting an e-mail attachment. Please note the fact that each time you select one single file. This means that it can be a long, tedious process if you have a lot of files, so you should look for a server that provides an interface where you can select more than one file, which will save you a great deal of time.

There are Web hosting servers that enable you to upload a Zip file that contains your entire Web site. What are the stages in this process? You build a Web site on your PC. You compress the whole Web site as one Zip file (all the folders and all the files), then you upload the Zip file to the server. The server opens the Zip file and structures the Web site (folders and files). Read carefully the instructions in the site for this method and pay special attention to **how** you must create the Zip file.

Tips for effectively uploading the Web site

◎ **Check how much storage space you will need** – by checking the size of your Web site folder on your PC. How do you do that? In Windows Explorer, highlight the folder that holds your Web site (HTML pages, pictures, etc..), right click with the mouse on that folder, and from the pop-up menu select "Properties" (the last option at the bottom). One of the properties is Size (third from the top).

◎ **Open another e-mail account in one of the free e-mail servers, even if your Web hosting server offers an e-mail services**. It's best to choose an e-mail server that does not obligate you to use the account every 30 or 60 days.

Please note that during the registration for a free Web hosting server, you must provide an e-mail address. This e-mail account must be active, which is a condition for continuing to host the Web site on the server. If you have an e-mail account on one of the free servers (such as Hotmail), even if you change ISPs, your e-mail address will be accessible. Use the e-mail address for all the Web site needs: working with the service suppliers connected with the Web site (the hit counter, forum), and for any additional services that you choose to put on your Web site.

◎ **Give as many real details about yourself as possible when registering with a Web hosting company**. Look for the privacy declaration of the Web hosting server which declares that they undertake not to pass on your details to a third party and not to make any use of them except for the needs of your Web site. Even if you have decided not to provide real details in the registration form, it's important that your e-mail address be real and accessible, otherwise they will close your Web site.

◎ **Does your Web site really belong on the Internet?** Before you put your Web pages on the Internet, it's a good idea to examine this point. Would you visit a Web site like this if it wasn't yours? If the answer is yes, ask yourself if you are proud of it. Can you show it to your Mom? To your classmates? Never present content (text and pictures) on your Web site that you would not be prepared to show to your Mom! Never display content on your Web site that you are not prepared to talk about in your school. Put on your Web site content (text and pictures) that you would be proud to show your mother and material that you are comfortable talking about and, preferably, are also familiar with.

◎ **Anything that is illegal outside the Internet is also illegal on the Internet**. Never display on your Web site content that might be considered slander or libel.

Be sure that your content is legal and in the spirit of the law, otherwise you are opening yourself up to a flood of lawsuits that could entangle you for the rest of your life, and might even leave you penniless.

Copyrights on the Internet

Written texts are copyrighted whether you have found them in a book, a newspaper, a CD or another Web site. Graphics, music (including notes and lyrics), computer programs, pictures, films, works of art and the Web site design are also copyrighted. You must be aware of the copyrights on materials that you use. Just because you are in possession of certain content, it doesn't not mean you can disregard the copyrights. Infringing copyrights on the Internet is just like infringing copyrights outside the Internet. Precedents have already been set in the matter, so it's not worth getting into trouble.

All printed material is protected under the Copyright Law, including this book. The company's policy, as written at the beginning of this book is:

"All rights reserved. No part of this book shall be reproduced, stored in a retrieval system, or transmitted by any means, electronic, mechanical, photo-copying, recording, or otherwise, without written permission from the publisher…"

In other words, you are not allowed to plagiarize (which is in effect a form of stealing). However, if you want to copy a short section, for example a paragraph, you can do so and note in fine print or in a footnote the source of the material (the title of the book and the publisher). With regard to larger sections, you must submit a proper request.

And what about your copyrights? The moment your Web site is on the Internet, it is exposed to the entire world, and people may copy content from it including text and graphics. If someone makes personal use of the materials from the Web site (for example, if someone copies a picture that you created in order to print a greeting card, or someone copies an article for the purpose of doing his homework), it is not a problem. The problem is created when these materials are used to make another Web site. There is no process for registering copyrights on Web site content, so this right exists without the need for any registration from the moment that it is published. If someone really wants to use the content and the files from your Web site, you can not stand in the way. The question is how much you are prepared to invest in finding plagiarisms and in bringing those cases to court, two actions that can cost a great deal of money.

A common mistake is thinking that if the sign © does not appear, then the content can be used freely. Furthermore, if the source of the material (a picture, music file and so forth) is unknown, that doesn't mean that it can be used freely.

Building a site by means of a wizard

Building a site by means of a wizard (a software that guides you step-by-step through the process of building the Web site) is similar to building a Web site with an HTML editor like FrontPage or DreamWeaver, except that instead of building the Web site on your computer, you build it online by filling in forms and answering questions directly on the server's computer.

The disadvantages of using a wizard:

1. Building a Web site with a wizard restricts you to the possibilities enabled by the wizard. In other words, you must adapt your content to the template that the Web host server makes available to you.

2. The Web site is built online – you must be connected to the Internet. If you have a slow connection, the process may take a very long time, aside from the cost.

3. You must prepare all the components of the Web site (text, pictures) ahead of time, otherwise the work becomes a nightmare: you get online, you get stuck (a picture is missing), you log off, you find/create the missing item, you get online again, get stuck again, log off again, find/create the missing item...

4. Since the Web site is built on the server's computer, there is no copy of the Web site that you built on your computer. If you decide in the future that you don't like the server and you want to transfer to another server, you'll have to build your Web site from scratch.

The advantages of using a wizard:

1. You don't have to know HTML.

2. While a building wizard helps you build the Web site easily without any knowledge, you should know that building wizards vary from server to server and so do the results. Some of the wizards are very simple and easy to work with, but the results they produce are also very simple and can only contain pictures and text according to a set structure. Some of the wizards can give far better results, but sometimes working with them is very complicated.

Conclusion

You can build a Web site that's totally cool, absolutely awesome and a few other superlatives, but if it's hosted on a slow Web hosting server that tends to crash, or one that's flooded with pop-ups – visitors won't return. Your Web site needs just a few seconds to impress the visitor. The following chapter will walk you through the process of promoting your Web site.

Choosing a Web hosting server is not something to be done lightly. And once you have found a good home for your Web site, start promoting it anywhere and everywhere, not just on the Internet.

Promote your Web site

The Web site is on the internet – now what?

Announcing your Web site or – how do you advertise/promote your Web site?

OK. So you've built a Web site and it's on the Internet. But aside from you and your parents, no one else knows about it... That's a difficult problem. A Web site that has no visitors is the nightmare of every Web site owner.

There are several ways to publicize the Web site, but don't rush to advertise it if it isn't finished. No respective Web site portal/index will add a Web site with empty/incompleted pages. Even Internet surfers who come to your site while it's under construction will be irritated and disappointed by its poor content and incomplete design, and that will just about guarantee that they'll never return.

Warning

If the Web site really isn't good enough, it is better to wait and NOT publish it until you improve it and save yourself the heartache and disappointment.

Try to examine your Web site as objectively as you can. If it wasn't your own site, would you be impressed by it? Be honest with yourself.

Try to get opinions from people you know, both young and old, that use the Internet, like your parents and/or relatives. Sit them down in front of the Web site and observe them silently. Let them work, don't explain to them what to do (I assume that you won't be able to explain what to do to every visitor who enters your Web site, right?) Your job is just to watch and take notes. Watch them as they browse through the site; try to get inside their heads, see how they act, try to understand where they get stuck and why, what bothers them, what they don't find and where they hesitate – this is your control group. Listen to their comments. You don't have accept their comments, but it is your duty to listen. Don't try to argue with them and "teach" them how to work on the Internet. They learned about the Internet by working on it and they are trying to use the knowledge they have already accumulated while visiting your Web site.

If it's hard for you to decide, send your Web site address to some close friends and ask for their criticism/opinions. Another way is to request criticism of the Web site on Web site critique forums or Web site builders' forums. View the criticism and the comments you receive as an opportunity to learn and to improve.

Forums (chats)

There are thousands of forums on the Internet that deal with every subject on earth. The participants in these forums are active Internet users and therefore they are also an excellent target audience.

A forum is an excellent place to announce your new Web site to everyone, but be careful that you aren't too "brutal" in spreading the message. Out of the thousands of existing forums, find the ones that deal with the subject matter of your own Web site. The participants in that forum will have an interest in your Web site. The forum administrators do not like advertising, so publicize your Web site in a manner that won't annoy them and the regular forum members. In the Web site builder forums your announcement will almost certainly be deleted, but it's worth a try there as well.

If you send out a request for help or for a critique of the Web site it will usually ensure a flow of visitors, as well as criticism (positive or negative). Some of the popular forums have a bulletin board or special forum for various advertisements where you can advertise your Web site safely.

In principle, you can also leave a message about the existence of your Web site in forums that are not connected with your Web site subject matter. Before you write something in the forum, it's a good idea to read some of the messages and see what the atmosphere is in the group. It is also a good idea to read the "opening letter" or "Webmaster's message" in order to learn the forum rules. In any case, each time you write something in the forum, answer a question or respond on some subject, leave a link to your Web site, even if the Web site is not exactly connected with the forum subject.

There will definitely be several forum administrators who will view this as advertising and will delete your message, but don't spend too much time worrying about that. You may write to the less visited forums who wish to get traffic from all sorts. Write a simple, friendly message and don't forget to leave a link.

Banners

A banner is a strip of advertising placed on various Web sites, which contains text, pictures or animation, with the aim of attracting the viewer's attention. Clicking on a banner connects the viewer to the Web site of the advertisement.

Advertising space can be purchased for placing banners. The cost of the space depends on: the popularity of the Web site, the placement of the banner on the page and its location within the Web site (on the main page or on the internal pages), the amount of time of the advertisement is displayed and other parameters. In any case, it is quite expensive.

You can also have advertising banners for FREE. The first method is to join a Web site that deals with exchanging banners among the various sites (banner exchange). Read the membership conditions carefully. If you do so, you'll understand that the ads of the "big" advertisers will appear on your Web site far more that your advertisements will appear on their Web sites, if at all!

A second possibility is by exchanging banners with another Web site. Find Web sites on your subject that are prepared to include a link to your site, in exchange for a similar link from your site to theirs. You advertise another Web site and another Web site advertises you. It is, of course, desirable that the Web sites have something in common, but it's not essential and sometimes it's preferable to find a Web site that complements yours and not one that competes with it.

There are advantages and disadvantages to using banners. On the one hand, the existence of a banner to your Web site from another Web site increases the chances of bringing visitors to your site, but on the other hand, your Web site becomes a kind of advertising Web site and you must devote space to advertise others.

Web site rings

A Web site ring or advertising ring is a chain of Web sites that are linked and share a common subject. The idea is that Internet surfers who are interested in a particular subject can move from Web site to Web site within the ring and know that all of them deal with the same subject. The advantages of the method are clear from the user's point of view. It's worthwhile for you, the Web site owner, because there is mutuality – just as you connected to other Web sites, other Web sites are connected to you. Additionally, a Web site ring does not require the same amount of space that would be necessary if the Web site owner wanted to link all the Web sites in the ring by means of banners or even by regular links.

Written and broadcast communications

Today, in every respectable medium (newspapers, television, radio) you can find a news/items/articles about the Internet. Take a look at your newspaper and you will find sections, and even supplements, devoted to the Internet. There are special magazines and journals on the subject. There are also special programs on TV and radio devoted to what is happening on the Internet. A news item or article about the Web site in the media is an excellent way to expose the Web site to a new Internet surfing public.

All journalists who deal with the Internet have an e-mail address, which appears next to their names, in the printed newspaper or on the newspaper's homepage. Publishing the e-mail address invites readers to write, to respond and to report on new subjects and Web sites. Even programs in the broadcast media have Web sites you can e-mail a letter to tell them about a new Web site. Try it – it can't hurt and it's FREE.

Advertising by e-mail

There are e-mail distribution lists (newsletters) on almost any subject imaginable. The top part of the e-mail contains a message on the relevant subject to the addressees on the distribution list, followed by the content of the advertisement. The disadvantage of this type of advertising is that most users don't read past the message that interests them, and thus the chance of them reaching your advertisement is negligible, and if you have to pay for it – it really is not worthwhile.

You can also advertise by means of FREE e-mail. Prepare a well written letter and send it to everyone in your address book. Ask them to forward it to everyone in their address books, and there's a chance that the message will reach more and more people.

Include in your name and a link to your Web site to every message sent from your e-mail. Someone who reads the message might want to know who wrote it and the link can bring visitors to your Web site.

Change line, change banner

On many Web sites, there is an option to change a link with "change line". It is FREE. If you encounter this, leave a link to your Web site. It's a good idea to come up with a cute, catchy sentence that will make viewers curious to check what kind of Web site is behind it. Similarly, there is also "change banner". There are Web sites on which you can change the banner in the special advertising cube. If you encounter this, there is no reason why not to change the banner and link it to your Web site – again, it can't hurt.

Guest book

If you visit a Web site, leave a response in the Web site owner's guest book. It is FREE. Even if you have nothing important to say, write something nice and congratulate the owner or wish him good luck. He'll definitely come to visit, and maybe others who read the message will also visit… you have nothing to lose – you're already there.

Sometimes, on small Web sites, the forum operates as a guest book. The rule is, if there's no guest book on the Web site, leave a message in the forum.

Registering the Web site in the search engines and indexes

Most of the homepages (the page that opens in the browser when you connect to the Internet) of most Internet surfers are portals, indexes, and search engines. Most people don't type in the address of a Web site that they want to visit in the browser's address line.

Most of them look for it by name on the search engines (that's why you need a good, catchy name), and also by subject (for example, they remember that there's a great Web site about…). It is, therefore, a very good idea to distribute the Web site on the search engines and to register it on the various indexes.

If you have a Web hosting server that you're paying for, check the contract to see whether it is supposed to promote the Web site. If it is, give the contact person the relevant details (Web site name, short description, keywords, etc.). Check to see if he really did the work and after about a month check the various indexes to see that the Web site is really there. If your Web hosting server does not promote your Web site, you can do it yourself by means of software that you pay for, or by manually entering the Web site in each one of the search engines.

Usually, on the main page of every search engine or portal there is an "Add Web site" or "Submit a Site" link. Clicking the link opens a form for registering the Web site. There are places in which registration is not done by means of a form, but rather by e-mail. In order to understand exactly what they want, read the instructions carefully.

When registering your Web site, you will generally be asked for personal details: address, telephone number, fax number and so forth. In some cases, there's no need to give all the details, but some of the search engines don't accept the registration if one of the lines in the form is empty. There are sites in which the important lines in the form are marked, so be sure to fill those in.

Before you begin working, draft yourself a list of actions you need to take:

1. Copy the address of your Web site to the top of the page and make sure that it's the correct address. Remember, one small mistake in the Web site address and all your work will be for nothing!!!

2. Type in your e-mail address and make sure it's written correctly. It's best for this to be the e-mail address that you opened for the purposes of the Web site.

3. Choose keywords – at least five words, you can also use phrases – preferably words that are popularly used on search engines and are connected with the subject matter of your Web site. Study the various search engines and look for their search logic.

4. Write a short description of your Web site. Explain the content of the site and how it can contribute to those who visit it. The description should be genuine and comprehensive. Don't make baseless declarations, because then there's every chance that your Web site will be disqualified.

5. Decide on the Web site classification according to its content.

6. Keep the draft file in your own computer in the Web site folder, from which you can copy (Ctrl+C) and paste (Ctrl+V) the details into the appropriate place on the various forms.

There are Web sites (portals, search engines…) that will notify you, by e-mail, when your registration form has been received. Other Web sites do not inform you and there's no clear way to know whether the application was accepted. There are also Web sites that will notify you that the Web site was inserted in the index – and there are those that don't. It's a good idea to check whether your Web site was registered and placed on the various indexes a month after registration. You can send another application for registration to all the search engines on which the Web site was not registered, but don't flood those sites with messages, which could annoy someone and hurt your Web site's chances of getting into the index lists.

If you do not succeed in registering the Web site, try improving it (by adding content, changing the design) and then register it again.

Significantly improving your Web site, or adding or changing content, presents an opportunity to update all the search engines that offer an option to update a registered Web site, in the hope that a new registration will lead to upgrading the placement of the Web site on the index.

Staying in touch with visitors

After you have worked so hard and distributed the news of your Web site's existence, visitors begin to arrive. It's important to stay in touch with them:

◎ Offer visitors the option of joining the Web site's distribution list to receive periodic e-mails, which will inform them of what's happening on the Web site (new sections, additional services, etc.).

◎ Make sure that your e-mail address appears in a prominent place so that visitors will be able to send you e-mail. This is the easiest way to stay in touch with visitors to your site.

◎ A forum is also a way to keep in touch with visitors to the Web site. Before you build a forum, think about who it's meant for. Who will manage it and how many participants will take part in it?

Conclusion

The promotion work will never end. This will be a continuous effort to let every body know about your Web site. Keep your mind open: try to evelute where to spend less time and effort and get more visitors, search for new advertising tools and think about promoting your Web site outside the Internet.

J

jpg (file extention), 54

L

Language, 32
    Server side, 159
Law, 133, 179-180
Layout of a Web page, 111-116
Line break, 65
Link, 53-68
    a Text to an Image, 55-58
    an Image to an Image, 74-75
    color, 60
    without underline, 126-127
Linux/Unix, 159
Loading time (Web page), 139

M

<meta />, 31-32
Maintenance (Web site), 139
Materials, 20
Media, 187
Menu, 117-127
    Create, 119
Microsoft Internet Explorer, see Internet Explorer
Microsoft Notepad, see Notepad
Microsoft Windows Explorer, see Windows Explorer
Microsoft Word, 135
Minimal loading time, 140
Mom and Dad, 20
Mouse cursor, 60
    Hand, 60

N

Name
    Web page, 32

[End of Index]